D0192638

Words of Praise for *It's All About Him,* by Denise Jackson

Denise's story is an inside perspective on the results of the ups and downs of fame. Her personal struggles with life's ordinary and extraordinary consequences, her passion to have a stronger marriage, and her desire to have a closer walk with God make for a truly inspiring life.

Carrie Underwood
2005 American Idol Winner
Recording Artist

"Behind every great man is a great women" may be a cliché, but it's still true. Alan Jackson, like me, would not be where he is today without the love, support, and sacrifice of a praying wife. The Jacksons have been blessed far beyond the success and fame everyone sees. Those of us who know Alan and Denise, know that they have been tested and have learned some difficult life lessons and are stronger for them. This excellent book tells their story and will be an encouragement to you.

Michael W. Smith
Singer/Songwriter

It's All About Him is a transparent story of a woman who moved from fear to faith by the grace of God . . . and with a lot of encouragement from her girlfriends. I believe Denise's book will be encouraging (even life-changing) for many women. I, for one, would stand in line forever to hear stories like this one—well told and with conviction. Her personal, relational and spiritual growth is compelling. She's a delight. I loved it!

Mary Graham
President, Women of Faith®

Denise Jackson's book is sensitively, honestly, and beautifully written and should be read by every married couple. It is a story of God's restoration and healing in marriage, the power of forgiveness, and the courage to face your own faults with a repentant heart. Alan and Denise Jackson's lasting love encourages all of us that our marriages are worth fighting for, no matter what it takes. They chose the hard and narrow road that leads to life and countless people will benefit from their decision.

Stormie Omartian
Best-selling author

We have known and loved Denise and Alan for many years. As with many of us in our industry, they have experienced life's temptations and the complications that have had a dramatic affect on their marriage. At the lowest point in their marriage, Denise cried out to God. Her book tells of how God answered her prayers and the healing process to their marriage began. We admire Denise for sharing her personal story that is rich with a message of a faith that has allowed her to "Stand By Her Man." With God all things are possible. We believe that, too.

George and Nancy Jones
Recording Artist & Member of the Country Music Hall of Fame
Wife and Personal Manager
(Married 24 years)

This book is proof that money and success do not bring happiness. I'm so thankful that Denise, in her honesty, has shared her story of how Jesus is what makes life worth living. We hear of so many broken relationships. It is a blessing to finally read a story of real people making it day by day, trusting God, and finding joy and love in the midst.

Denise Jones
Point of Grace

Denise Jackson has told her story with courage and honesty. We were inspired and blessed as we read it. What a wonderful example of the way the Lord Jesus takes the "mess" of our lives and makes a message that will bless others and glorify Him!

Ricky Skaggs and Sharon White
Grand Ole Opry Members
(Married 26 years)

Without pretense or embellishment, Denise Jackson has shared a story so honest and transparent that, should other young women find the courage to face life like she has and find their true identity in the great I Am, many marriages could be salvaged and families transformed.

Gloria Gaither
Author, Lyracist, Communicator

It's All About Him

Finding the Love of My Life

DENISE JACKSON
WITH ELLEN VAUGHN

FOREWORD BY
Alan Jackson

THOMAS NELSON
Since 1798

NASHVILLE   DALLAS   MEXICO CITY   RIO DE JANEIRO

© 2007 by Denise Jackson

All rights reserved. No portion of this book may be reproduced, stored in a retrieval system, or transmitted in any form or by any means—electronic, mechanical, photocopy, recording, scanning, or other—except for brief quotations in critical reviews or articles, without the prior written permission of the publisher.

Published in Nashville, Tennessee. Thomas Nelson is a trademark of Thomas Nelson, Inc.

Published in association with the literary agency of Wolgemuth & Associates, Inc.

Thomas Nelson, Inc., titles may be purchased in bulk for educational, business, fund-raising, or sales promotional use. For information, please e-mail SpecialMarkets@ThomasNelson.com.

Unless otherwise noted, Scripture quotations are taken from the HOLY BIBLE, NEW INTERNATIONAL VERSION®. © 1973, 1978, 1984 by International Bible Society. Used by permission of Zondervan Bible Publishing House. All rights reserved.

The "NIV" and "New International Version" trademarks are registered in the United States Patent and Trademark Office by International Bible Society. Use of either trademark requires the permission of International Bible Society.

Scripture quotations noted NLT are from the *Holy Bible*, NEW LIVING TRANSLATION, © 1996. Used by permission of Tyndale House Publishers, Inc., Wheaton, Illinois 60189. All rights reserved.

ISBN 978-1-59555-149-8 (trape paper)

Library of Congress Cataloging-in-Publication Data

Jackson, Denise J., 1960–
    It's all about him : finding the love of my life / Denise Jackson with Ellen Vaughn ; foreword by Alan Jackson.
        p. cm.
    Includes bibliographical references (p.   ).
    ISBN 978-0-7852-2776-2 (hardcover)
    1. Jackson, Alan, 1958—Marriage. 2. Jackson, Denise J., 1960—Marriage. 3. Country musicians' spouses—United States—Biography. 4. Country musicians—United States—Biography. 5. Christian biography—United States. I. Vaughn, Ellen Santilli. II. Title.
ML420.J14J33 2007
782.421642092'2—dc22
    [B]

                                                                    2007011528
Printed in the United States of America

10 11 12 RRD 6 5 4

Recognition

WITH GRATITUDE . . .

To my Lord and Savior Jesus Christ, for planting the desire in my heart to write this book, and in Your perfect timing, faithfully leading me every step of the way. I give You all the glory and honor for this and every blessing in my life. I pray that every reader will come to experience the same passionate love relationship with You that I have found.

To my parents, Dan and Nell Jackson, for your unconditional love and for taking me to church every Sunday of my childhood. I have been blessed to have you as my parents. I love you dearly.

To my siblings, Ron, Jane, and Danny, for always believing in me and encouraging me. Your presence in my life has helped shape me into the person I am today. I love you.

To my mother-in-law, Ruth, and my father-in-law, Eugene, for always loving me as a daughter and for raising your son to be the godly man that I get to share my life with.

To my sisters-in-law, Diane, Cathy, Carol, and Connie: Your early influence on Alan has helped to make him the sensitive, compassionate, and caring husband and father that he is. Thank you all.

To my sisters in Christ, Jane, Liz, Beth, Kim, Joy, and Beth:

You were heaven-sent angels, whose love and support helped me through the toughest days of my life. I love you all.

To everyone at Thomas Nelson: Since our very first meeting, your excitement and belief in this book and its message have been overwhelming and a real confirmation to me that our partnership was Spirit-led.

To Tim DuBois, whose decision to sign Alan to Arista Records gave me the platform to tell my story. I am forever grateful to you.

To my business manager, Debbie Doebler, and my assistant, Jerri Cook, thank you for graciously accepting all the added responsibilities that have come with this book project. I appreciate you more than you know!

To Robert Wolgemuth, my friend and now my literary agent, for awakening my heart and soul to the truths of God's Word. Thank you for recognizing God's story of grace and restoration in my life and marriage, and for guiding me through the steps to bring this book to fruition.

To Bobbie Wolgemuth: Your radiance and love for the Lord is a perfect example of what Christ means when He calls us to be "the light" in a dark world. I am forever grateful for your intercessory prayers on my behalf.

To Ellen Vaughn: What an incredible experience this journey with you has been! Your brilliant writing has brought a level of excellence to this book that I never could have achieved on my own. You have turned an otherwise daunting and intimidating task into a fun-filled adventure! It is an honor to have your name on the cover of this book with mine.

To my three precious angels, Mattie, Ali, and Dani: Being your mother has been the greatest joy of my life. You continue to amaze me every day, and make me so proud. I love you with all my heart.

To Alan, the one and only love of my life—what an adventure this life with you has been! Thank you for showing me by your example how to go after my dreams. You are my greatest inspiration. I love you more than words can express.

To my three precious daughters,
Mattie, Ali, and Dani:
My heart's desire for each of you is
that you will experience the same passionate love
relationship
with Christ that I have found.
It truly is all about Him.

And to Alan:
To recover something of great value
after it has been lost
makes me treasure it even more.
You, my darling, are my greatest treasure.

Contents

CONTENTS

BY ALAN JACKSON

"If I had it to do all over, I'd do it all over again,
If tomorrow I had one more chance to begin,
I'd love you all over again."

Early in my music career, I wrote those lines in a song as a tenth anniversary gift to Denise. They were sincerely written from a younger, less-experienced perspective. But I really couldn't appreciate the complete meaning of those simple words until I'd shared almost three decades on a roller-coaster road of life with this amazing woman.

Denise and I began our journey together as teenagers and have watched and helped each other grow into more balanced and healthy people. She was a skinny cheerleader and homecoming queen for Newnan High School, a prime catch for small-town Newnan, Georgia. I was a young boy with hormones and an unclear understanding of true love. But we made it to the altar, and twenty-seven years later, I see more clearly the deeper reasons I first fell in love with her.

Not long after we married, I came home one day with a high-performance off-road motorcycle I had taken on trade. Denise asked if she could ride it. I tried to explain that this was not some typical little scooter. But she hopped right on and took off like a pro across the pasture joining our home. She's a rare combination: a gorgeous blonde with a "tomboy" attitude, who can make homemade biscuits just like my mama's.

I have watched this woman give birth to three daughters with no medication and never utter a sound. I have watched this woman of Southern grace, charm, beauty, talent, and integrity stand in the shadows of my overwhelming career and success while quietly serving as the rock I lean on day after day. I have watched her grow from a young girl who looked at me as part husband, part father figure into a beautiful, confident woman, wife, and mother.

Denise and I look back at the meandering path that has led us to this point in our life together and realize that all the wonderful moments, tragedies, disappointments, challenges, good and bad decisions have given us the opportunity to grow, heal, and develop as human beings and as children of God. We have experienced so much together. I'm so proud of her for putting our story into words, and so thankful that she has found a platform by which to live, and that her spiritual connection with God has truly blessed our lives and enabled us to survive so much.

There are many people, every day, who overcome more difficult challenges and hardships than you'll find in this book. But

I believe and hope that this story, without all the celebrity pros and cons, can easily be appreciated and adapted within any relationship. When I first read it, I could not stop turning the pages even though I know how the story ends! Exhausted from tears and laughter, inspired by Denise's strength and ability, I sat down and wrote a song of the same title—"It's All About Him"—to include with this book, hoping musically to add a little icing to an already uplifting story.

Images from our lives have always found their way into the words of my music, so I'll end this foreword by quoting one of my more recent songs that mirrors some of the same feelings that I wrote about in the song for our tenth anniversary, but written a million miles later!

"Remember when 30 seemed so old
Now looking back, it's just a stepping stone
To where we are, where we've been
Said we'd do it all again
Remember when."

I love you, Nisey!

A CINDERELLA STORY?

Livin' on love, buyin' on time
Without somebody nothing ain't worth a dime
Like an old fashioned story book rhyme
Livin' on love
It sounds simple that's what you're thinkin'
that love can walk through fire without blinkin'
It doesn't take much when you get enough
Livin' on love

Alan Jackson, "Livin' on Love"

In some ways my life feels like a fairy tale. I grew up in a little brick house with a gravel driveway in Newnan, Georgia. My daddy was a mailman. As a small girl I'd help my mother can green beans from our garden. I never dreamed that one day I'd live in an immense castle, showered with jewels by a handsome prince.

But that's what happened. Today tour buses pass the perimeter of our gated estate; people hang out the windows and take pictures of our mansion. Private planes, boats, and dozens of

1

cars stand ready to take me wherever I want to go, anywhere in the world. Three lavish vacation homes are staffed and available to enjoy at any time. Employees cook, clean, shop, and run errands for me.

I've been photographed in shimmering designer gowns on more red carpets than I can remember. I've spent time with actors, musicians, celebrities, and presidents. Reporters have interviewed me, eager to portray my private life for newspapers, magazines, radio, and television. Strangers often ask if they can have my autograph, or if they can have their pictures taken with me.

Why have I received all these benefits?

It's certainly not because of me or anything I've done. It's because I'm married to a country music superstar named Alan Jackson. Alan's award-winning, multiplatinum albums and his enormous career success over the last two decades have made him wealthy beyond his dreams; he's a celebrity whose fans adore him.

Because of our relationship, I receive these gifts as well. Out of Alan's graciousness and love for me, he has showered me with extravagant pleasures I haven't earned. I am rich—because of him.

Riches Anyone Can Have

Recently it's struck me how all this so closely parallels my relationship with Jesus Christ. I enjoy *spiritual* riches, not because of who I am or what I've done, but because of who God is and what

He's done. I'm rich in love, joy, and peace because I'm in an intimate relationship with a gracious God who loves me just as I am.

Obviously this parallel isn't exact. As Alan would be the first to say, he's human, full of flaws, weakness, and sin. So am I. We've gone through hard times, when each of us hurt the other. We've struggled in our love and commitment. We've fallen apart, separated, and come back together again. We've experienced the raw fact that wealth and fame really don't buy joy and peace.

We've learned in hard ways what is truly important: the priority of faith and family and the ties that bind us to the God who is always faithful, even when we are not.

That's why I've felt that perhaps it's time to share some of our journey. I don't know why you've picked up this book. You may be a fan of Alan's, and you're curious about his private life. Or maybe you've never heard of Alan Jackson and couldn't care less about country music . . . but you're curious about how God really works in people's lives, and how He might change yours.

Wherever you're coming from, our story is here to let you know that regardless of your situation, you can have the very richest blessings we enjoy. This is because the best assets aren't houses, planes, boats, cars, and diamonds that only the wealthy can possess. The very best gifts in this life are absolutely available to everyone.

Recently I met a woman who asked if she could take pictures of our estate. She was a Sunday school teacher, and she'd been telling the kids in her class about how Jesus said that He was preparing mansions in heaven for them. Since these kids had never laid eyes on a mansion, she wanted them to see pictures of one so they could better visualize the wonderful splendor of Jesus' promise.

I'm grateful for our beautiful home. Every time Alan and I drive into its big gates, we're floored that we actually get to live in such an incredible place. But it's made of bricks and mortar, and it will one day crumble. Christ's *heavenly* mansions will be more beautiful than we can imagine, and they will last forever. And they're available not just for the select few who make it big in this world, but for all who look to Jesus.

Better Than Material "Stuff"

I've learned through a lot of tears, over a lot of time, that possessions alone will never satisfy the hunger we all have inside. The only thing that can fill us up to overflowing is a real relationship with Jesus. That's not just nice religious talk. It's true. While material stuff is great fun, and I enjoy it and try to share whatever I have, I could give it all up tomorrow. But I could never give up Jesus, and more important, He will never give up on me.

Softly and tenderly, He calls each of us, His arms flung wide to hold us tight. He can give us real joy, true peace, and fulfillment forever. This isn't about religion or going to church or looking holy or trying to do all the right things. It's about being in an unbreakable bond with Jesus, living with Him in a cherished connection of love. He longs to bless us abundantly, beyond our wildest dreams.

As is pretty obvious, I'm no theologian. This book isn't a sermon on prayer, God's will, forgiveness, trials and temptations, or any of the other big topics on which it touches. I'm not trying to instruct anyone as if I'm an expert; many excellent authors have written with great insight about these subjects.

But I do know what I know. I'm like the blind man Jesus healed in the Gospel of John. When he was questioned as to exactly *why* this miracle had happened, he said, "I don't know!" Then he went on, "One thing I do know. Once I was blind, but now I see!"

That's a little bit like my story in this book. One thing I do know: Even though I had all the material things we chase after in this world, I once was miserable, full of uncertainty and fear. But now I have real joy and peace!

This transformation is why I have felt so strongly about writing this book. A life lived in the sweet riches of God's amazing grace is far better than any so-called fairy tale you could ever imagine. I know this firsthand. So can you.

It's all about Him.

Chapter 2

LITTLE BITTY BEGINNINGS

A good ol' boy and a pretty little girl
start all over in a little bitty world
a little bitty plan and a little bitty dream
it's all part of a little bitty scheme

Tom T. Hall, "Little Bitty"

It all started with a little bitty look, when I met Alan Jackson at the Dairy Queen in Newnan, Georgia. It was a warm Sunday night in 1976, and after the local Baptist churches in town finished evening services, all the teenagers went out for ice cream. I was sixteen years old, green eyed, my long, blonde hair parted in the middle just like all my friends.

But somehow Alan picked me out of the crowd. We were all chatting and laughing, and suddenly this tall, blond guy was standing at our table. He was looking down at me in a sort of sly way, and then he flipped a penny down my shirt. Smooth move.

Though I'd seen Alan at school, he was two years ahead of

me, and he went to a different church, so we'd never met. He sat down and talked for a while, and then he ambled away. He was nice, but I didn't think much about him.

Much later, the rest of us said good-bye as we headed toward our cars. I popped open the door of my mother's old brown LTD and slid onto the vinyl seat. I started the engine and pulled out of the parking lot, thinking about what I'd wear to school the next day and wondering where that penny had ended up.

> I SCREAMED AND NEARLY DROVE OFF THE ROAD, MY HEART IN MY THROAT, AND THEN SLAMMED ON THE BRAKES AND WHIRLED AROUND.
>
> IT WAS ALAN JACKSON . . . AND HE'S BEEN SURPRISING ME EVER SINCE.

Then I heard an odd, rustling noise in the back, and all of a sudden this long, lean, blond person popped up from the backseat, where he had been lying down, waiting for me. I screamed and nearly drove off the road, my heart in my throat, and then slammed on the brakes and whirled around.

It was Alan Jackson . . . and he's been surprising me ever since.

Newnan, Georgia

Actually, what was surprising was that we'd not really met before. Newnan, Georgia, was not exactly a booming metropolis. It was the county seat of Coweta County, about forty miles outside Atlanta. Founded in 1828, it had been the home of lawyers, doctors, and merchants whose income relied on slave-grown cotton.

During the Civil War, when my great grandfather was a Confederate soldier, the Southern cavalry defeated the Union Army in the nearby Battle of Brown's Mill. When I was young, it wasn't uncommon to see Confederate flags in the back windows of pickup trucks around town. In fact, there weren't a whole lot of people in town from north of the Mason-Dixon Line when I was young. And if people did move in from up north, it was immediately obvious by the strange way they talked.

Given those Confederate roots, it's redeeming that Newnan was also the site of the trial of the first white man in the South to be condemned to death for murder by the testimony of African Americans, two men who had witnessed the crime. Newnan's famous 1948 trial provided the story for the old movie *Murder in Coweta County*, starring Johnny Cash, June Carter, and Andy Griffith.

Andy Griffith would have fit right into Newnan. It was a bit like Mayberry. The courthouse was in the center of the town square, with shops and small businesses surrounding it. Pillared antebellum homes sat comfortably on the dogwood-lined streets. We never locked our doors during the day, and in the summer we only latched the screen doors at night. Most people there were interconnected; even if you didn't know someone personally, you had heard of him or her. And if your mama didn't know what you were up to, you could be sure she'd find out pretty quickly from any number of sources around town.

So even though I didn't really meet Alan Jackson until that

summer night at the Dairy Queen, I'd known about him for years. My twin brother had ridden motorcycles with Alan, and they had played on a youth basketball team together for a season. But I hadn't paid much attention. Maybe I thought that somewhere way far back in our tangled Southern roots we were related, since my maiden name was Jackson, too, and our fathers had both grown up in western Georgia. (Recently one of Alan's fans researched both our fathers' genealogies back to the 1100s; he found that we come from opposite branches on the Jackson family tree and in fact are *not* related. For the sake of future generations, let's just say we were relieved.)

Big Fish, Small Pond

Alan had made a big splash in our high school when he was the male lead in his senior play, but I didn't see the performance. And even though I could tell he was a persistent guy with a good amount of self-confidence, I wasn't particularly drawn to him. He called me a couple of times after that night at the Dairy Queen, but I just wasn't interested in going out. Maybe it was his hair. It was short, as his daddy insisted, parted on the side, and kind of awkwardly unstyled and wavy. (You can tell that at age sixteen I wasn't evaluating male relationships by particularly deep qualifications.)

Back then I was one of those "golden girls" that high school girls love to hate. Cheerleading captain, homecoming queen, #1 position on the tennis team, straight-A student, you name it. I'd always had a boyfriend by my side since about the fourth grade, and at Newnan High School, I was a big fish in a small pond.

You would think with all those accomplishments, I would have been a pretty confident person. But like a lot of teenage girls, I might have looked good on the outside, but I was a little lost on the inside.

In some ways life was very secure. I had a brother, Ron, who was twenty-one years older. As a toddler, my older sister had called him Bubba, her version of "brother," because she couldn't say Ronald. We all called him that forever after, although I looked up to him almost as a father figure. My sister, Jane, was seven years older than me. My twin brother, Danny, and I were a late surprise and focal point from the time we were born to my middle-aged parents, who had thought that their family was complete.

Church was the center of our social life. We were there Sunday mornings, Sunday evenings, and Wednesday nights for prayer meeting. I went to the same old brick high school as my older brother and sister, and it was assumed I'd go to nearby West Georgia College as well. Almost everyone I knew

> [ALAN] CALLED ME A COUPLE OF TIMES AFTER THAT NIGHT AT THE DAIRY QUEEN, BUT I WASN'T PARTICULARLY INTERESTED IN GOING OUT.
>
> MAYBE IT WAS HIS HAIR. IT WAS SHORT, AS HIS DADDY INSISTED, PARTED ON THE SIDE, AND KIND OF AWKWARDLY UNSTYLED AND WAVY.

dated and married people from Newnan, and raised their children there too. Life seemed to follow an expected pattern, never discussed, but known by all.

Family Matters

My parents grew up during the Great Depression. They were both hard workers and wanted to give us more than they had had. I never doubted their love . . . but they came from a generation that didn't necessarily communicate big dreams to their kids. Life was a matter of working hard and doing the next right thing. There wasn't much discussion about new ideas or personal feelings. Brainstorming at the dinner table about our life goals and ambitions was not something that I remember. We just took each day as it came, not really focusing on the future. Their focus was on getting through the work week and having money left on Friday to buy groceries. Because of that, I often felt like I didn't have the direction I so desperately wanted.

As a teenager, I interpreted this lack of specific guidance as a lack of love. It wasn't, of course, but I didn't understand that not having heartfelt conversations with my mother had more to do with *her* childhood than with how she felt about me. Born in 1920, she probably didn't get the depth of emotional nurturing that she needed, even though her parents loved her and did the best they could. For my mother, the growing-up years were more a matter of survival; her parents simply did not have time to focus on communicative, creative parenting with each of their thirteen children.

Even though I always knew that they loved each other, I rarely saw my parents demonstrate that love in front of us. I often wished that they'd express their love and affection in words and gestures more than they did.

I was a daddy's girl, a pleaser. My father was one of seven brothers. When their father died young, the two oldest and two youngest boys stayed in school, while the three boys in the middle had to go to work to support the family. So my daddy had to quit school in the eighth grade. He got his GED later on, but he never had the education to pursue his big dreams.

Instead, he worked hard to provide for us. He was a postal carrier and left the house very early each morning to deliver mail on rural roads in Coweta County. He'd come home in the afternoons, change clothes, and leave to work on the spec houses that he built and put on the market for extra income. By the time he came home at eight or nine in the evening, he was exhausted.

Though my father was interested in hearing about my day, I longed for a deeper kind of communication. I wanted my accomplishments—good grades, honors, special recognitions—to catch his attention. Perhaps I felt that if I was remarkable enough, I would get confirmation—and the "I love yous" that I craved—from both of my parents.

Like many teenaged golden girls, I was a mixed-up combination of outer confidence and inner turmoil. I had a smile for everyone, and I turned handsprings and led cheers on the football field. I was elected student body president. I felt good when other people thought I led a charmed life. But at home, sitting at the dinner table with my own family, I longed for real communication and an emotional connection I could not define.

Anything but Typical

It wasn't surprising that I always had a boy by my side. Even at the tender age of sixteen, I was defining my worth by how I looked, what I did, and who I was with. So I dated boys who did well and looked good, like the football quarterback. I wasn't impressed with a guy like Alan Jackson, who didn't play school sports and only cared about getting to a job so that he could earn money to buy and renovate cars.

But then, a few months after we first met, I happened to see Alan at a friend's house. He was with a date, and so was I, but he asked if I'd like to go for a quick ride in his little 1955 Thunderbird convertible. It was gleaming white, a vintage sports car he and his daddy had painstakingly restored, and Alan looked like he'd been reconditioned too. His blond hair was now parted in the middle, blown back with wings in the Farrah Fawcett style of the day, and he gave me a confident grin.

"Sure," I said, and we took off on a drive that lasted much longer than was polite. Then Alan went off with his date, and I went off with mine . . . but that little ride changed my mind about him, and the next time he called to ask me out, I was quick to say yes.

When he arrived to pick me up, he was in a big four-door Thunderbird sedan. I asked him if it was his mother's, and he laughed. Here he was, seventeen years old, and he had two cars, not because they had been given to him but because he had earned the money to buy them. We went to a movie in Atlanta, since Newnan had only one movie theater, with one screen—

and then to the Steak 'n Shake for burgers, fries, and milk-shakes. It was a typical small-town teenaged romance, with a twist . . . because anything with Alan Jackson is far from typical.

Chapter 3

WHERE HE CAME FROM

❦

Where I come from it's cornbread and chicken
Where I come from a lotta back porch pickin'
Where I come from tryin' to make a livin'
Workin' hard to get to heaven
Where I come from, Yeah where I come from
A lotta front porch sitting
Starin' up at heaven where I come from

Alan Jackson, "Where I Come From"

Alan was the youngest of five kids, the only boy. His daddy was a Ford mechanic, a man of very few words, who lived right, worked hard, and cared for his family. He also did untold acts of kindness for others that we didn't discover until his funeral in 2000, when dozens of people recounted his quiet impact on their lives.

Alan's parents had married when his mother was sixteen. She quit school to marry, and Alan's grandfather gave the teenaged couple his new twelve-by-twelve tool shed as their first home. They rolled it onto their property on big logs. As the kids started arriving, they were a bit crowded for space, so rooms were added to accommodate the growing family. There was one small bathroom for seven people, and for years Alan's bedroom was the hallway, with everyone passing through all the time. For Alan, it was like *The Waltons*—both of his grandmothers lived within one hundred feet of his home, his cousins were right down the road, and the Jacksons set a tone of hard work, temperance, and security, with everyone around, all the time.

In the beginning of our relationship, I'd go to Alan's for Sunday dinner, and his four older sisters, their husbands, and all their kids would be there. From the beginning, Alan's mother was always sweet and talkative; she made me feel right at home. I knew his daddy liked me too, but Daddy Gene was a very quiet man. After Alan and I had been dating for about a year, I commented to Alan that his father had never said my name, nor ever really talked to me.

Alan told his mother what I'd said. The next time I arrived for Sunday dinner, Alan's dad looked straight at me, nodded his head, and said, "Denise." That was it. Not "Hello, Denise," or "How are you?" Just my name. And for him, that was a stretch.

Seeds of Dreams

Alan inherited some of his dad's shy nature, but more of Daddy Gene's love for cars, his ability to make things run, his care for others, and his diligence. By the time Alan was twelve, he had his first job, working at a shoe store on Saturdays. He saved every dollar he earned, picking up other odd jobs along the way, rolling the coins he earned from his tips at the locally famous Sprayberry's Barbeque Restaurant. Later he worked as a furniture store delivery boy. And when he was fifteen, he had saved enough to buy his first car, that snowshoe white 1955 Thunderbird convertible. He had an unusual work ethic for a teenager.

He also had an unusual gift, his uncanny ability to duplicate sounds. If he was riding in the backseat of a car, he might cup his hands over his mouth and imitate a police siren, and whoever was driving would pull right over, or at least look in the rearview mirror. He scared his coworkers when he delivered furniture with them by making loud train sounds just as they were crossing the tracks. His animal imitations were pretty amazing as well.

More on point, he had a keen ear. He and his sisters

> ONE NIGHT ALAN'S FATHER WAS SITTING, SILENT AS USUAL, WATCHING *HEE HAW* WITH THE REST OF THE FAMILY. BUCK OWENS WAS SINGING A COUNTRY BALLAD, AND DADDY GENE TURNED TO ALAN. "YOU COULD DO THAT," HE SAID.

had grown up singing in youth choirs, and his mother—whose maiden name was Musick—sang beautifully as she went about her work in the house. And though Alan's daddy never sang, he always put gospel music on their stereo on Sunday mornings as everyone was getting ready for church.

This was back when the variety show *Hee Haw* was popular on national network television. Each broadcast featured skits and appearances by major country singers. One night Alan's father was sitting, silent as usual, watching *Hee Haw* with the rest of the family. Buck Owens was singing a country ballad, and Daddy Gene turned to Alan. "You could do that," he said.

It wasn't exactly a big watershed moment or a word of prophecy . . . but since Alan's daddy rarely spoke, let alone gave career direction, Alan remembers that comment to this day. He says it planted a small seed, one that grew into a big dream inside of him.

In between all his odd jobs, Alan partnered with a friend, Eddie Norton, who played guitar, and they started singing at events around town. When he was sixteen, Alan's parents gave him a guitar, and he taught himself to play approximately four chords, which was just about all he needed at the time.

More and more people began to notice his rich, unusual singing voice. Friends started asking him to sing at parties and weddings. Eventually a man named Cody Deal heard Alan sing at a wedding and asked him to join a band he was forming. So Alan became the lead singer for "Dixie Steel," named after a box of nails found in the basement where they practiced. They played around Newnan and Atlanta for several years, even coming in second place at the infamous Marlboro Country Music contest sponsored by an Atlanta radio station.

Young Love

Meanwhile, when Alan and I look back today, it's hard to remember our dating life. All we know is that there is absolutely no way we would want our three daughters to date and get serious and marry at such a young age. Alan says that maybe they can date when they're about thirty or so . . . but back in the distant mists of our own youth, we fell in love when we were just teenagers, as little as we knew what love was about.

Years later, after Alan had achieved superstar status in the country music world, we were interviewed by *Life* magazine for a cover story on celebrity marriages that had endured over decades. I was thrilled, because we were to be featured with heads of state and political leaders, as well as other entertainers. When the magazine was published, there we were with dignified couples like King Hussein and Queen Noor of Jordan, President George H. W. and Barbara Bush, Vice President Al and Tipper Gore, and *60 Minutes* journalist Mike Wallace and his wife, Mary.

I was feeling good, excited about being in such distinguished company . . . until I looked at Alan's quote that the magazine had chosen to use as the bold headline for our interview. Alan had been asked what initially drew us together and sparked our grand love story. He had responded, "I just wanted to get into her britches." (This is *not* what George Bush had said about Barbara!)

I don't think that I will *ever* fully recover from reading that quote. But at any rate, his remark reminds me what a miracle it is that our love grew and matured over the years, because we were so young when it began. And because of that, we inadvertently started some unhealthy habits early on in our dating life.

Because Alan was such a provider, he took on a kind of father role for me. If you ask him today about our early years, he'll say that he half-raised me. I don't know if that's quite true—or maybe it's just half-true—but he was certainly the decision maker in our relationship in terms of making plans, buying cars, eventually paying for my college education, leading any adult aspect in our relationship. I gladly handed such things over, because I felt like Alan was much more experienced and confident than I was. But this uneven dynamic would create problems years later.

For my part, maybe as a reaction, I didn't want him to be too sure of me. So I'd try to keep him a little off balance. In high school I acted very high-schoolish, breaking things off with Alan every once in a while and dating the quarterback to make Alan jealous. Then he'd show up at football games with a date, and I'd have to face the stands, cheering for the crowd, watching Alan with some other girl. He always found some way to impress me and get me back . . . and then he'd do whatever he could to make *me* feel insecure.

To use today's psychological terms, I think the word to describe it would be *codependency*. We attempted to meet some of our needs in ways that weren't healthy, mature, or mutually satisfying. There was a certain "relationship addiction" for me in particular. As the years went by, I needed Alan in order to feel good about myself, in the same way that people who are addicted to alcohol have to have a drink in order to face their day.

So, woven in the tapestry of our love story, there were some dark threads that would get knotted later on. There were also many bright threads, sweet times, and shared hearts. And early on in our relationship, Alan's strength and love bolstered me through the hardest time I'd yet known.

Chapter 4

SHOCK

I need some sunshine on my face
To help me dry my eyes
I need a blue sky over head
So I can clear my mind

Alan Jackson, "Rainy Day in June"

It was Valentine's Day, 1977. I was at a friend's house when I got the phone call. My twin brother, Danny, sixteen years old, had been riding his Honda 125 motorcycle, his blond hair blowing back in the cold wind. He didn't have his helmet on. He was less than a quarter mile from our house when a young driver approached from the other direction. The driver was traveling west; blinded by the setting sun, he turned and never saw Danny on his motorcycle until he hit him.

Danny had no time to react. The car crashed into his left side, knocking him off the motorcycle and up into the windshield of the car, over its hood, and into the ditch at the side of the road. Still conscious, he was in so much pain he wished he was dead.

My Twin Brother

Danny and I had spent all our growing-up moments together. I was a classic tomboy when we were young, wrestling and running with my twin brother everywhere we went. We'd ride bikes with no hands, seeing who could beat the other. We played football with the neighborhood boys, climbed trees, and rode our Honda cycles all over the front and back yards. Daddy would take us to his little pond in the country, where we'd fish and skip rocks on the surface of the water.

As we got older, I resigned myself to being a girl, and our interests diverged. But we still had that inexplicable closeness of twins, and now that Danny just might die, my brain could barely take it in.

My mother and daddy were already heading to the hospital. I called Alan, and he came to get me.

My older sister, Jane, was living in Carrollton, about thirty miles west of Newnan. Alan and I called her and told her that we were on our way over. We made it to Carrollton in record time. When we got out of Alan's car, he held me up as we walked to Jane's door. Jane and I held each other, crying. The teakettle, left boiling, whistled on the stove. Alan went into Jane's bedroom, grabbed a suitcase out of the closet, and started packing it with clothes, makeup, and toiletries.

24

We threw ourselves into the car. By the time we arrived at Newnan Hospital, the ambulance had left again. The Newnan doctor had told my parents that the only thing they could do was amputate Danny's leg. It was too mangled to save, held together only by a thin piece of skin. Our older brother, Ron, insisted that they transport Danny to a larger hospital in Atlanta. Maybe more could be done for him there.

We took off for Atlanta. When we finally got there, Danny was lying on a gurney in the emergency room. He had been given morphine for his pain, and was drifting in and out of consciousness. He told us not to look at his injuries, but we couldn't help it. His hand was the size of a basketball, every bone crushed. His leg was bloody and mangled, with a piece of bone sticking out.

Danny went into surgery, and my parents made us all go home. They knew it would be many hours before we had any news . . . and perhaps they wanted to protect us from what might happen.

> WITH MY TWIN BROTHER NEAR DEATH, BROKEN AND BLOODY, I WAS SHAKEN TO MY CORE. I PRAYED LIKE I'D NEVER PRAYED BEFORE, ASKING GOD TO SAVE DANNY'S LEG AND HIS LIFE.

Thankfully, Danny made it through surgery. But his battle had just begun. The next few weeks and months were a blur for us, and excruciating for Danny.

If I was a golden girl, Danny had been the masculine version of the same thing. A football player who was quite popular, he always had a girlfriend and had an energetic, happy-go-lucky personality. At the time we didn't know that the accident would change his life's direction.

Danny's accident was the first time I'd been confronted with trauma and crisis. I had prayed all my life, and accepted Jesus as my Savior at age twelve. I had gone to Sunday school as long as I could remember, and I knew all the right answers about life and death and heaven. But with my twin brother near death, broken and bloody, I was shaken to my core. I prayed like I'd never prayed before, asking God to save Danny's leg and his life.

To Walk Again

During the two months Danny was in the hospital, Alan drove my mother and me to Atlanta every day. Mama wasn't comfortable with the traffic there, and Alan took over the driver's seat for her. It was his natural place for all of us. Even though he was young and we had dated less than a year, Alan was the type of person who took care of everyone else.

After sixty-three days of lying flat on his back in traction in a hospital bed, Danny finally came home. His leg was saved. Gradually, he learned to walk again. But the accident crushed his spirit more than his legs. He couldn't go back to football or the rosy future he'd always assumed he'd have. As he would be the first to say all these years later, he chose a path that spiraled downward. Though he eventually overcame this way of life, his despair after the accident pulled him toward bad choices, unhealthy friendships, and failed relationships.

My relationship with Danny had always been a source of

strength and security. My twin was part of who I was. But as the months and years went by, particularly after the trauma of Danny's accident and the shock waves it sent through my family, Alan became my all in all. My friendships with other girls dropped away. My family no longer seemed invincible, like my image of Alan. Bit by bit, my life and thoughts focused on one thing. Alan: it was all about him.

Chapter 5

SURPRISES

༄

Remember when we vowed the vows
and walked the walk
Gave our hearts, made the start, it was hard
Alan Jackson, "Remember When"

Over the next few years, whenever Alan and I were out in his little Thunderbird convertible, people told us we looked like a dream couple. In fact, a local store used the car—and us—as models for an advertising campaign. Today I look at that faded black-and-white photograph, and it makes me smile. Both of us look so young and eager, driving toward a future we couldn't yet see.

We were each other's first true love, but we had never talked about marriage. We were too young.

On Christmas Eve my freshman year of college, we were at my mother and daddy's house, sitting on the sofa next to the Christmas tree. Alan handed me a beautifully wrapped gift a little smaller than a shoe box. I smiled; I never knew quite what to expect from him. One Valentine's Day he had given me a powder blue car fender—romantically wrapped with a big red bow—to replace the fender that had been crumpled when my VW bug was attacked by an angry cow.

But this box was too small to hold any major car parts. I carefully opened it. Inside was another wrapped box. Alan grinned as I opened it. Inside was a smaller package. Then there was another. And another. The last one was a small, black velvet box.

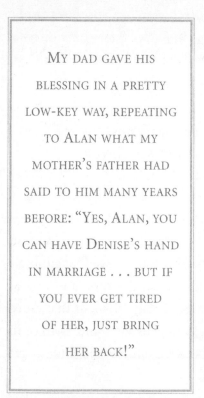

MY DAD GAVE HIS BLESSING IN A PRETTY LOW-KEY WAY, REPEATING TO ALAN WHAT MY MOTHER'S FATHER HAD SAID TO HIM MANY YEARS BEFORE: "YES, ALAN, YOU CAN HAVE DENISE'S HAND IN MARRIAGE . . . BUT IF YOU EVER GET TIRED OF HER, JUST BRING HER BACK!"

Oh, that's so sweet, I thought. *It must be a necklace.*

I eased open the velvet lid. Inside was a gleaming, perfect, half-carat diamond solitaire. I stopped breathing.

"Denise," Alan said softly, "will you marry me?"

I could not speak. I was shocked. I was too young. Too afraid. Too breathless.

"Well," Alan said, sensing that maybe things weren't going quite according to his plan, "you don't have to tell me now . . ."

I managed to find my breath. "Yes!" I said. "I just don't want it to be right away."

My Parents' Blessing

As surprised as my parents were, they were all for it. They had seen how responsible, loving, and determined Alan was. After all, he had worked, saved, and gotten a bank loan in order to give me a car for my high school graduation. Most twenty-year-olds just didn't do things like that. My dad gave his blessing in a pretty low-key way, repeating to Alan what my mother's father had said to him many years before: "Yes, Alan, you can have Denise's hand in marriage . . . but if you ever get tired of her, just bring her back!"

Mice on the Cake

The following December, when I was nineteen and a sophomore in college, we were married at the First Baptist Church in Newnan. Although I had grown up in Unity Baptist Church, we had started attending Alan's church and decided to be married there. The church was decorated for Christmas with two evergreens at the front, both with white lights. The windows were filled with magnolias and greenery, with baskets of red and white flowers on either side of the altar. The massive crystal chandeliers were dimly lit for the evening ceremony, and the church was filled with friends and family.

Alan wore a black tuxedo with a black bow tie—no Stetson—and according to the wedding announcement in the *Newnan Times-Herald,* I wore "a formal gown of imported nylon organza"—I never knew that nylon was imported—"with pearled and bugle beaded Chantilly lace." The local newspaper went on and on: "The long fitted sleeves trimmed with matching lace ended in points at the wrists and the A-lined skirt swept to a full chapel train. The bride wore a fingertip length mantilla and carried a linen handkerchief edged with tatting made by the groom's maternal grandmother."

Just after our vows, Alan turned to me and sang "That's the Way," a wedding song by Pat Terry.

With this ring I thee wed and I give to you my life
Mine is yours and yours is mine
And we can live that way forever
With this kiss we will seal that we now are man and wife
Two in one, one in two
That's the way it's got to be

He may not have been nervous about getting married, but he was nervous about singing in front of our two hundred guests.

My parents hosted our reception. Since this was a Baptist church wedding in a dry county, there was no alcohol. (Neither of our fathers would have approved of it anyway.) We had home-made cheese straws and mints, mixed nuts, and a traditional white wedding cake with a little plastic bride and groom on top. They looked slightly confused, standing there in the icing, unsure of their future. The groom's cake was chocolate and decorated with red icing poinsettias and, oddly enough, a mouse bride and a mouse groom on top, standing under an arbor of icing mistletoe. I'm not sure what the little mouse couple had to do with anything, but we were young, and maybe we thought they were cute.

We spent our first night in Atlanta at the Peachtree Plaza Hotel. We walked a few blocks to a Steak and Ale to eat. Even though my sister had packed us a treat box from the reception, we were starving for real food. The next day we headed to north Georgia in a Thunderbird demonstrator that Alan had gotten from his job selling cars. It had a blue leather interior and push-button controls, and we cruised along in style, listening to Ronnie Milsap's latest hit, "Nobody Likes Sad Songs."

We arrived at our destination, a lodge that claimed to be the southernmost ski resort in the United States. Accordingly, it had absolutely no snow, real or artificial. We tooled around the area, visiting antique shops, and ate at the locally famous Dillard House, which serves Southern food family-style. This means that you sit with people you don't know, at large tables, passing large bowls of food, just like you were family. Alan, never one for chatting it up with strangers, absolutely hated it.

Getting Started

As we headed back to Newnan for Christmas, I was excited about being married. I felt that Alan would be a good husband, and believed that I had made the right decision. We were both so young, though, that I still can't believe no one encouraged us to wait awhile. If I had it to do over, I still would have married Alan, but I would have lived on my own first. I went straight from living at home, dependent on my parents, to being married to

Alan, dependent on him . . . though I wasn't a slouch, since I was caring for our home, taking a full load of college classes, and working part-time as a bank teller.

Everyone enters marriage with expectations, or at least unexpressed assumptions. Our marriage models were our parents, who had worked hard, kept their vows, and sustained marriages that lasted for a lifetime. So we both believed, without even articulating it, that marriage was for life.

Like many young girls, I had a bit of a Cinderella complex. If my part was simply to play the role of the girl to be swept off my feet by the handsome prince, I looked to Alan to make everything work in our life together. Not that he was born to royalty—far from it—but Alan had the knack for making things happen. He seemed to instinctively envision what could be and move toward that goal. I knew that by his side I would be going somewhere.

People always told us we were made for each other. And in some ways, perhaps that increased my dependence on Alan. I didn't feel complete without him; I relied on him for my sense of well-being. This dependence grew over the years, and in some ways my personal growth stalled. I wasn't thinking about growing as a person, nor was I growing in the only thing that could truly sustain me, a faith in Christ. I was just thinking about what would make me happy. And the more I sought happiness for its own sake, the more it eluded me.

Chapter 6

HIGH HOPES

⟪ ❦ ⟫

My first love was an older woman
There's been many since
But there'll never be another
Built in 1955, snowshoe white, overdrive
I never should've sold her, I'll always love her . . .

Alan Jackson, "First Love,"

As Alan and I started our new lives together, he proved his love for me by letting go of the "older woman" he had treasured since he was fifteen.

By this I mean, of course, the little white Thunderbird that Alan and his daddy had restored so carefully, the car that symbolized his youth, that car that he truly loved as much as a human being really can love a car. At any rate, he sold his T-bird for ten thousand dollars, which became the down payment for our first house.

Our church was getting ready to tear down a small, turn-of-the-century home across the street to make room for additional parking. Alan struck a deal with the church leaders to give us the house if we paid to have the lot cleared. After the movers removed the house's foundation and roof and cut it in half, we moved our "new" house to six acres in the country, where we had it reassembled and restored.

Alan was an incredibly hard worker and a great provider, but his sense of humor was a little twisted. One night he was working a late shift, and I was at home, relaxing after a hard day. I had filled our old bathtub with hot water, and I was mostly submerged, eyes closed, blissfully enjoying the moment.

Then I heard footsteps in the house. I'd lost track of time, but it seemed too early for Alan to be coming home from his second-shift job. And usually he called my name when he came in.

Still in the tub, I froze. The steps drew closer to the bathroom, and then they stopped. I watched in horror as the old knob on the bathroom door began to turn, turn, turn. Then the door opened a crack. A hand reached slowly in and snapped off the light switch, leaving me in total darkness.

The only thing that saved me from having a fatal heart attack at that moment was the fact that I had recognized my husband's long hand as it reached in the door. I jumped out of the tub, pulled a towel around me, and started screaming at Alan to *never, ever* do something like that again.

Later someone actually did break into our home and steal almost everything we had. Because of Alan's night hours, there was no way I was going to stay there any longer. We sold that little house and bought another one in town. A year later, we bought the next house, renovated it, and repeated the process. Meanwhile I worked at the bank and took a class load that would allow me to complete my degree in three years rather than four.

Second Grade All Over Again

I finished college, got my teaching certificate, and eventually taught second and third grades at Atkinson Elementary School, the same school I had attended as a girl. Some things there had not changed. For example, I partnered with one of my former teachers, but I couldn't bring myself to call her by her first name. So I called her Mrs. Mann, just like I did when I was eight years old.

The kids, however, seemed quite different from my memories of my elementary friends. They were much wilder than we had been. I came in on the first day of school with all my handmade learning games, neatly organized and laminated. My lesson plans were ready to roll, the classroom was creatively decorated, and I knew this was going to be the best learning environment these kids could hope for.

By the end of the first day, however, the room was in shambles, my games were strewn everywhere, I was a mess, and I didn't think any of us would make it through the year.

But we did, and I grew to love the kids, particularly the ones who came from disadvantaged backgrounds. They were so hungry for love and attention, just as we all are.

Sweat Equity

Alan had dropped out of college so he could work full-time to support us while I was still in school. Over the years, before he broke into the music business, he sold cars, built houses, did carpentry, and took tests to be an air-traffic controller, a postmaster, and an airline baggage handler, though none of these jobs was his life's ambition. He drove a forklift at the Kmart warehouse, a huge distribution center that supplied the surrounding stores with merchandise. On the weekends he played at clubs and at special events with Dixie Steel.

Alan quickly had enough of unloading boxes at the Kmart shipping dock. When we'd talk about our future, he already knew that he would love to sing for a living. He had seen how big goals could be realized when two of his friends from Newnan, Doug Channell and Bubba Whitlock, had dreamed of becoming pilots. It wasn't the norm among our small circle of friends back then to leave town to pursue your dreams; most people stayed in Newnan, some doing what their daddies had done. But Doug and Bubba had worked hard, gotten their pilots' licenses,

> OVER THE YEARS, BEFORE [ALAN] BROKE INTO THE MUSIC BUSINESS, HE SOLD CARS, BUILT HOUSES, DID CARPENTRY, AND TOOK TESTS TO BE AN AIR-TRAFFIC CONTROLLER, A POSTMASTER, AND AN AIRLINE BAGGAGE HANDLER . . . HE DROVE A FORKLIFT AT THE KMART WAREHOUSE.

signed with an airline, and taken off for the wild blue yonder. *If they can get to where they wanted to go*, Alan thought, *I can do it too.*

But it wasn't until we bought tickets to several country music shows in nearby Franklin, Georgia, that he really started to seriously consider music as a career. The first show we attended featured "The Kendalls"; another was "The Whites," a father/daughter group that included Ricky Skaggs's wife, Sharon. Alan loved these shows. We also saw George Strait, a real cowboy, whose career and songs greatly influenced Alan back then . . . and Alan still holds George in extremely high esteem today.

In early 1985, one of my closest friends I had taught with, Margie Moore, urged me to join her in becoming a flight attendant. She had left her teaching job the previous year to work for Piedmont Airlines. I had never even flown in an airplane, so becoming a flight attendant sounded exotic and sophisticated. Plus, the pay was higher, and the hours shorter, than teaching.

So the next thing I knew I was in Greensboro, North Carolina, for three weeks of flight training with Piedmont Airlines. This was back in the old days of air travel, long before stringent security and the tight rules of the post–September 11 world. Back then, flying still had a certain panache to it . . . particularly for me, since this was so foreign to the down-to-earth world in which I'd grown up.

Around this time, Alan bid the Kmart a less-than-sad farewell and quit his night job. We sold our house, and while I was away for flight training, he moved to nearby West Point Lake, taking up residence in an old trailer we used as a weekend getaway.

Every morning he got in our little boat and zipped across the lake to the marina where he was working. In the evenings he came back and put a burger or two on the grill. Sometimes he had a melody in his head all day, and that night he'd play the guitar and work out the lyrics. It was a lonely time for him, but one in which he had unprecedented time and solitude to develop his songwriting skills.

A "Chance" Encounter

Looking back, I can't help but see God's hand in providing this quiet time for Alan, as well as giving me the airline job. Becoming a flight attendant gave me opportunities to literally try my wings, to grow in independence in ways that I wouldn't have down on the ground at Atkinson Elementary School. It also provided the doorway, oddly enough, for Alan's big break, career-wise.

One day, after I'd completed my training and was flying regular routes, I was in the Atlanta airport. As I walked toward the gate, I saw a man standing in the boarding area. It was country superstar Glen Campbell. He was dressed casually, traveling with several guys, probably his tour manager and band. I recognized him immediately; he looked just as I remembered him from *The Glen Campbell Goodtime Hour* on TV when I was a child. He'd also been on *Hee Haw* and was one of the best-known singers in the world. Songs like "Rhinestone Cowboy" and "By the Time I Get to Phoenix" started running through my head. All this took about a second, and then I knew what I had to do.

I wasn't the kind of person who felt comfortable approaching celebrities, but I knew this opportunity wasn't going to come by again anytime soon. I took a deep breath and went over to him. He was chewing gum and smiled when I approached. I assumed that was because he was getting ready to laugh and tell me to go away.

"Mr. Campbell," I said, "may I talk with you for a minute?"

There was plenty of time before his plane.

"Sure," he said. I told him that my husband wanted to get into the country music business, and asked what advice he might have.

He paused a moment, then asked if my husband wrote songs.

I thought of Alan, sitting up late every night with his guitar, making memories into music, and love into lyrics.

But all I said was, "Well, yes, he does."

Glen said, "That's good." He gave me a business card with the name "Marty Gamblin" on it. "This is the man who runs my music publishing company. Have your husband send his songs to Marty to see what he thinks."

I held on to the card like it was a passkey to our future.

Years later, when Glen wrote his autobiography—*Rhinestone Cowboy*—he said that he gave that same advice to plenty of others. For whatever reason, most of them never followed through—or if they did, the songs were just plain unusable.

But, as Glen put it in his book, "[Denise's] husband wasn't like most songwriters."

Within two weeks of my "chance" meeting with Glen Campbell in the Atlanta airport, Alan was standing in Marty Gamblin's office.

After listening to Alan's plea, Marty graciously committed to help him and act as his manager, even though he continued to work full-time running Glen Campbell's music publishing company. Alan returned to Newnan. We packed up all our possessions (which didn't even fill a small U-Haul), and away we went, driving toward our dreams in Music City.

Our first-ever home away from Newnan was an apartment complex near the Nashville airport, which made sense, given my flying schedule. What didn't make sense when we arrived was the dirty parking lot with rusty cars up on concrete blocks, the wild kids running around, and the swimming pool that was just a dry concrete bowl, empty except for a puddle of scummy water and a dead rat lying in the bottom.

So began our grand new life in Nashville.

Chapter 7

DAUNTING DISAPPOINTMENTS

❦

I've played for empty tables and chairs
For drunks that don't listen and crowds that don't care
Been told countless times Boy you ain't goin' nowhere
To do what I do

Tim Johnson, "To Do What I Do"

There's usually a big difference between what you imagine will happen when you go off to pursue your grand dreams and what actually takes place. Alan and I both knew that Nashville wouldn't exactly welcome us with open arms and a key to the city, but still, our early days there were pretty depressing.

We stayed in that dank little apartment for two months, which was exactly two months too long. Drug deals were going down in the hallways; strange men came and went at all hours of the night. I wasn't comfortable going to the laundry room if

Alan wasn't home. There was a fire in one of the apartments, and then a domestic shooting in another.

After that, I was by the front door when Alan got home: "I love you to pieces, honey," I told him, "but I am *not* staying here."

Thankfully, God had prepared a place for us. A little notice had just gone up on the bulletin board in the employee work-

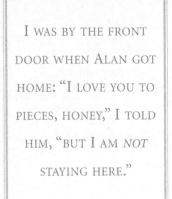

I WAS BY THE FRONT DOOR WHEN ALAN GOT HOME: "I LOVE YOU TO PIECES, HONEY," I TOLD HIM, "BUT I AM *NOT* STAYING HERE."

room at the Nashville Network, of a cozy basement apartment in a quiet, nice neighborhood, for $350 a month. We jumped at it. On our moving day, when we stopped at a 7-11 store on our way to the new place, a man saw our truck loaded with our old, battered furniture.

"Hey!" he shouted. "You just come from a yard sale?"

We hauled our hand-me-down furniture into the little apartment. It had brown shag carpeting that blended just fine with our old brown and orange patchwork sofa. In our bedroom, our mattress had belonged to Alan's older sister. We could see why she'd decided to give it away: it had a trench worn into the middle, and Alan's feet hung off the end. But at that time we were glad to get anything.

Alan, who is six foot four, had to sleep on it diagonally. Since he was heavy, I spent half the night trying to claw my way out of the "Alan trench," and the other half curled into a little triangle of space.

Busy Airports and a Lumpy Mattress

In order to have a regular flight schedule and not be on call, I had to be based in Washington D.C., which meant that I had to start and end my trips there. While other flight attendants bid for layovers in the most exciting cities, I just tried to get schedules that allowed me to spend as much time in Nashville with Alan as possible.

So I was getting up very early in the morning, flying to Charlotte, North Carolina, to make a connection, then to D.C., just to begin my scheduled flights. On the way home I'd run through airports to catch the late flight home to Nashville, Alan, and that lumpy mattress.

Alan would pick me up at the airport. Since this was before the tightening of airport security, he could just idle at the curb outside Piedmont arrivals, waiting for me to emerge. Our only vehicle at the time—a Dodge Transvan—happened to look a lot like the shuttle vans that transported travelers to and from their parked cars. One night Alan was waiting for me at our usual curb when a businessman opened the van's door and hopped into the front seat.

"To parking lot G, please!" he commanded.

Alan sat at the steering wheel, pondering whether he should take this guy for a little ride around the airport or let him go. In the end he informed the businessman that he needed to catch the *airport* shuttle, that Alan in fact was a private citizen waiting to pick up his wife. The man reluctantly got out. For our part at least we knew that if Alan's music career never took off, he could always get a job at the airport, driving a shuttle bus.

I loved flying. I enjoyed making passengers feel welcome and comfortable; I liked taking care of their needs. I loved getting to know the other crew members; there was a fun camaraderie between the flight attendants and the pilots. Though some of them partied together, I wasn't interested in getting together with anyone. I just enjoyed the meals out as a group, the laughter, sightseeing in places I'd never been (which weren't difficult to find, since I'd hardly been anywhere), and shopping (even though I browsed a lot more than I bought, since we didn't have much money).

Paying His Dues

In the flying world I felt competent and connected with others . . . but then I'd come home to Nashville and feel a bit disconnected from what Alan was experiencing in the music world. Much of it was pretty depressing anyway. One time I flew up to Canada to meet him at a gig somewhere. Alan's band was playing at a bar that was connected to a hotel. The floor was sticky with old beer and who knows what else. The patrons were drunk and rude, and most of them could not have cared less about Alan, the band, or music in general. They just kept downing drinks and coming and going from the strip joint that was next door to the bar.

In the music business, playing in these kinds of places to crowds that don't listen is called "paying your dues," and if anybody paid his dues, Alan did. He'd drive to a gig maybe six, ten, fourteen hours away, with the heavy music equipment loaded into a trailer he pulled behind the Dodge Transvan, which we jokingly called the "Country and Western Showbus." (Saying "country and western" is like saying "stewardess" instead of "flight attendant.")

Alan would unload all his stuff, do a sound check, play from 8 PM to 1 or 2 in the morning, inhaling dense clouds of smoke, then crash in a cheap hotel, get up the next morning, head for the

> IN THE MUSIC BUSINESS, PLAYING IN THESE KINDS OF PLACES TO CROWDS THAT DON'T LISTEN IS CALLED "PAYING YOUR DUES," AND IF ANYBODY PAID HIS DUES, ALAN DID.

next destination, and do it all over again. Even worse than that was having to play at the same dreary place for more than one night—at least going to a new place gave Alan some slight hope that conditions might be better at the next stop.

By the time he paid his band and the expenses, there wasn't much—if anything—left. Sometimes he even *lost* money. But even back then, he knew that murky gigs on the road would give him the experience that he needed for the bright future he was determined to reach. Meanwhile, he was writing songs for Glen Campbell's production company—for the grand sum of $100 a week.

The lonely nights of dark bars, stale pretzels, and sticky floors were so different from my earliest musical memories. I remember my mother's family reunions when I was a little girl. As I said earlier, Mother was one of thirteen siblings. All the Browns, large and small, would gather at an old Methodist church in the country, where earlier generations of Browns were tucked under warm, gray stones in the old cemetery.

Everyone brought picnic baskets full of crispy fried chicken and creamy deviled eggs. There were vegetables fresh from the garden, a rosy ham, sweet cornbread, baked beans, a snowy coconut cake, and crunchy pecan pies.

After we were full from the feast, we'd all gather around the old piano in the church fellowship hall. One of my aunts would play, and everyone would sing, with wonderful harmony, the great old hymns that were part of the ties that bound us together.

That rich fellowship was a far cry from Alan's drab life on the road and my hectic commutes from airport to airport. But nothing in our experience is wasted, and I know that God used that time in our lives in a variety of ways . . . ways I couldn't appreciate until many years had gone by, when I could see God's purposes in the rearview mirror.

At the time it was just plain hard. I remember paying our bills only to discover that there was nothing left, except two more weeks before the next paycheck would come. Each time I cried, Alan tried to cheer me up. He kept saying that it wouldn't be this way forever. But that didn't magically change our finances.

Sometimes we'd wonder what in the world we were doing . . . why we were putting ourselves in such dismal situations when we had families and friends who loved us and would have welcomed us back home with open arms. We often thought about all the warm fellowship and wonderful Sunday dinners we were missing at Alan's mother's house. Maybe all the stress and cold rejection just wasn't worth it.

My first-grade
school picture
(1966-67)

Alan's first-grade
school picture
(1964-1965)

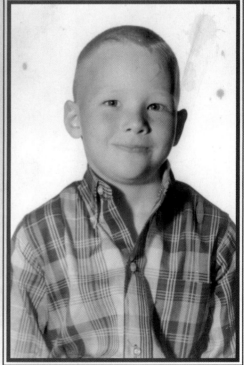

My Jr./Sr. Prom at Newnan High School (1977)

Alan and me with his beloved Thunderbird (1977)

Alan and me homecoming night at Newnan High School
before I was crowned queen. (1977)

Alan and me soon after we started dating

I was cheerleader captain my senior year (1977-78)

Our Wedding—December 15, 1979

My flight-attendant days at
Piedmont Airlines (1985)

#1 Party for "Here In The Real
World" single (April 1990)
Hope Powell Photography

My mother & daddy
with Mattie on her
first Easter (1991)

Alan and me at the White House
with President George & Barbara Bush (1992)

My brother Ron and his wife Debby

Big sister Mattie proudly holds her new sister, Ali (Aug. 1993)

Mattie, Ali and me with their miniature Mercedes (Christmas Day, 1994)

Our family celebrating Dani's arrival at Baptist Hospital (Aug. 1997)

My infamous short haircut (1998)
Photography by Pamela Springstein

December 15, 1998—Renewing our wedding vows at First
Presbyterian Church, Nashville. From left—Chip and Norma Jane
Peay, Tom and Jane Smith, our family, Mary Miller,
Bobbie and Robert Wolgemuth

But Alan never gave up. All the disappointments and challenges that we faced just made him more determined to reach his goal.

Hoping for the Best

We had given ourselves five years to make it in Nashville. If things didn't work out, then we really would go back home. Life there would be different from our big dreams, but it would still be good.

Thankfully, Marty introduced Alan to many people in the music business, like Gary Overton, Keith Stegall, and Barry Coburn. Like Marty, these guys played instrumental roles in Alan's career. I couldn't even begin to name all the wonderful people who did so much to help and promote Alan in those early days. We are forever in their debt.

For more than three years Marty did everything he could to spark record label interest in Alan. Time after time he solicited producers to record demo tapes

ONE EXECUTIVE LISTENED TO ALAN'S TAPE AND SIGHED. THEN SHE TOLD ALAN THAT HE JUST DIDN'T HAVE STAR QUALITY AND THAT HE SHOULD GO BACK TO GEORGIA AND GET A JOB DOING SOMETHING ELSE.

that he would then pitch to executives . . . in fact, every record label in town rejected Alan at least once. Some turned him down twice. One executive listened to Alan's demo and sighed. Then she told Alan that he just didn't have star quality and that he should go back to Georgia and get a job doing something else. Later, one label decision-maker actually agreed—verbally—to sign Alan. Marty, his wife Cherie, and Alan and I were so thrilled that we went out to a nice restaurant to celebrate. But the deal never materialized . . . and it was all so discouraging, to say the least.

Eventually Glen Campbell's music company financed a demo session that allowed Keith Stegall to produce a new tape of Alan singing a few songs that he had co-written. Marty pitched it to his friend Shelby Kennedy, who in turn shared it with his friend, Anthony Von Dollen. Anthony listened to the demo and then convinced Tim Dubois, head of Arista Records in Nashville, to hear Alan perform live in a showcase performance sponsored by Glen Campbell Publishing and Barry Coburn. (Barry would later become Alan's sole manager.) Tim was a songwriter himself, so perhaps he recognized Alan's depth and artistic creativity. He took a risk and signed Alan as the very first recording artist for Arista's new country division.

By this time more than four years had gone by in our five-year Nashville plan. We weren't kids any longer. I was twenty-nine, and we both felt that perhaps, with this new record deal signed, we could start a family.

To our surprise, I became pregnant right away. We were absolutely thrilled but weren't sure exactly what in the world we were getting ourselves into. Deciding to try to become pregnant was not nearly as scary as being pregnant. At the time, a flight attendant in my airline could work through her seventh month of pregnancy, and then had to take an unpaid leave of absence. We couldn't help but wonder what we would do about little things like insurance and money to buy groceries and diapers.

Half the time I was exuberant and happy. I felt great, and the pregnancy progressed wonderfully, even though I eventually had a little trouble in my maternity uniform, making my way up those narrow airplane aisles.

But the other half of the time I was gripped by a cold fear. What would we do if Alan's record failed?

We waited, hoping, even praying a little, though we had not even thought much about God or been to church since we'd moved to Nashville. There just wasn't time for it anymore, it seemed, and so, without realizing it, we were drifting from the moorings that had helped to secure us when we were young. Bit by bit, we were usually going with the flow all around us.

For example, Alan's new manager thought it would be wise to change Alan's name, considering that another country artist had a similar name. We considered John Alan …. John Hubert (both versions of Alan's grandfather's name), but in the end, we all agreed that he would keep the name he was born with. Thank goodness for that.

Names were one thing, but it was less amusing when they messed with his image. They didn't want it to seem like he was married. This isn't unusual; I've heard stories of performers' wives who were told by management to stay home, keep a low profile, pretend you don't exist. The presence of a wife might affect the new star's image as the latest new country sex symbol.

In our case, though, it didn't look like anything was going to happen to make Alan into a hot star anytime soon.

The Real World?

The first album was called *Here in the Real World*. Its first single was "Blue Blooded Woman," the song of a redneck man and his higher-class love.

Around this time Alan started going on radio tours, meeting disk jockeys and program directors, promoting himself and his new album. At this point image was everything. The idea was to look like a big star even if you weren't. We wanted people to see Alan arriving at the radio stations in a long, black limousine. Even if they had never heard of him, they'd think he was someone important when they saw him climb out of his stretch limo wearing his signature torn Wrangler jeans, his Stetson hat, and his custom-made cowboy boots.

The problem was, the radio stations just weren't going to fork out the bucks for a limo for an unknown like Alan Jackson. One station told Alan and his manager that they'd send transportation to pick them up at the airport . . . and it was a 1970 station wagon with wood panel sides. A station in another state sent an old VW hippie camper with flower decals on the sides and laminated kitchen cabinets inside.

Finally a radio station in West Virginia actually sent a limousine to pick up Alan at the airport. The only problem was it was ancient, with enormous mud-grip truck tires, and the entire rear end had been crumpled by a collision. The driver put Alan's luggage in the smashed trunk, but the lid wouldn't close. So he tied it down with a piece of twine and took Alan off to the station, traveling in style.

When "Blue Blooded Woman" was first released, Alan and I

bribed our friends Gary and Jan Overton to come over to our basement apartment. We promised them that we would order pizza if they would help us call various country radio stations across the nation to request Alan's new single. Gary was originally from New Jersey, so he called the Northern ones, requesting that they play "that great song from that new singer, what's his name, uh, Alan Jackson?"

Meanwhile Alan and I called the Southern stations. "Hi," I'd drawl. "I'm just calling to see if you could play that really great new song, you know, 'Blue Blooded Woman'?"

"What?" they'd say to me. "Blue Bloody Woman?? What's that? Who's it by?"

"Alan Jackson!" I'd say proudly.

"Never heard of him!" they'd yell.

Well, we didn't exactly send Alan's single rocketing up the charts. Neither did anybody else. We watched the country music charts obsessively. "Blue Blooded Woman" made its way up to number 43 . . . and then it absolutely died. Most radio stations in the country never even played it.

Chapter 8

DREAMS COME TRUE

⌗

Wish I were down on some blue bayou
With a bamboo cane stuck in the sand
But the road I'm on, don't seem to go there
So I just dream, keep on bein' the way I am

Sonny Throckmorton, "The Way I Am"

Even as Alan's first single shrank, the baby inside of me continued to grow. Arista got ready to release Alan's next single. I felt like time was running out. Typically a label will release two—or possibly three—singles from a new artist, and if they don't do well, you're done. Plenty of great singers are waiting in the wings, vying for their own chance for stardom.

"We're going to be living in a trailer on food stamps!" I'd say to Alan. "That's our baby's destiny!"

I was kidding, but my fears were real. What would really happen to us, and our baby-to-be, if the label dropped him?

#1!

The second single came out in early 1990. Like the album, it was called "Here in the Real World." I flew my usual routes with Piedmont, which had by now been bought by USAir, and came home to our little mismatched basement apartment with Alan's bittersweet song ringing in my ears:

> Love is a sweet dream that always comes true
> Oh, if life were like the movies, I'd never be blue
> but here in the real world
> it's not that easy at all
> 'Cause when hearts get broken
> It's real tears that fall . . .

Again, of course, we watched the *Billboard* charts every week, our stomachs in knots. The folks at Arista were doing all they could to fan the flame. Alan's song rose steadily in the charts. It got to the twenties and didn't stall. After all the years and tears and hopes and fears, were our dreams about to come true?

Yes.

Alan's song got bigger and bigger, even as my stomach swelled and I got bigger and bigger too. At the end of March, "Here in the Real World" hit number one on the country music charts. We could not believe it.

April 6 was my thirtieth birthday, and Arista threw a "#1" party for Alan. I have to confess that I had always had these mental pictures of myself as the lovely "star wife" if Alan ever made it big. Instead, *I* was big . . . seven months pregnant, like a swollen balloon, with fat ankles and a very large maternity outfit. Not exactly what I'd had in mind for our first taste of celebrity.

But even at that point, something had changed. We were treated differently. There was a certain excitement and energy in the room. Where did it come from? Record sales? Radio airplay? The scent of big money? Alan was the same as he'd always been, but now there was something intangibly powerful, seductive, and fun that followed him, and people suddenly wanted to be nearby.

Our phone began to ring

> I HAVE TO CONFESS THAT I HAD ALWAYS HAD THESE MENTAL PICTURES OF MYSELF AS THE LOVELY "STAR WIFE" IF ALAN EVER MADE IT BIG. INSTEAD, *I* WAS BIG . . . SEVEN MONTHS PREGNANT, LIKE A SWOLLEN BALLOON, WITH FAT ANKLES AND A VERY LARGE MATERNITY OUTFIT.

nonstop from well-wishers who were all of a sudden very interested in what was going on in Alan's career. Distant family members whom we'd never met came forward, hoping to connect with their long-lost relative. Word spread around Nashville about this hot new country singer on Arista Records. The buzz was big.

At first, it was so flattering to be recognized by admiring fans, and we both experienced a "honeymoon" phase when life could not have been better. We loved the kind attention, Alan's music was getting the kudos it had long deserved, and we both felt like our dreams were coming true. The celebrity lifestyle tasted quite sweet to both of us.

I didn't really analyze it all back then. Too much was happening all around us, and I was, of course, also preoccupied with what was happening inside of me. Even though the baby was due on June 8, she seemed quite content to hang out there, so we scheduled labor to be induced on June 19, two days after Alan got home from his weekend shows.

Labor of Love

Because I was having signs that labor might start sooner, while Alan was gone, I stayed on the couch the whole weekend, trying not to move, hoping that would keep the contractions from starting. Alan made it home on that Sunday night, and on Tuesday morning, the scheduled day to induce, I went into labor on my own.

It was disconcerting, but I wanted to make sure I looked half-decent for this momentous day. I was sitting at the mirror, putting on makeup, when Alan appeared with the video camera. "Okay, it's June 19," he narrated, sticking the camera in my face and then zooming in on my gigantic abdomen, "and Nisey's in labor!"

"Go away!" I said nicely. "Now!"

He loaded me into our Jeep Wagoneer, and we sped away to the hospital. My goal was to have the baby without medication, and with as little intervention as possible, as had been encouraged in the childbirth classes we attended. In our training, Alan had been instructed how to rub my back and make supportive comments and be totally compliant with the process. So I lay in the fetal position for hours, with Alan quietly feeding me ice chips when I asked—and only when I asked. I told him to shut the curtains and not to talk. Dr. Trabue came in every once in a while, and he finally told me that I could continue to labor for several more hours, or he could break my water and we would have a baby very soon.

I had wanted to go through the process without intervention, but this was getting to be a bit much.

"Break it!" I said.

We had not found out the baby's sex ahead of time. We wanted it to be a surprise. But unbeknownst to me, Alan had seen the hospital bassinet set up in the birthing room. The baby's little bracelet was already in it, ready for the birth, and it said "MALE" on it. So all day, Alan thought that the nurses had somehow known that we were going to have a boy. But he didn't tell me.

After hours of pushing, straining, and the loss of all dignity on my part, our beautiful baby finally arrived. Alan looked her over.

There's, uh, something missing, he thought. *She's a she!*

Later he asked the nurse about the bracelet that had said she was a boy.

"Oh," she said, "they're all labeled 'MALE' until after the birth. Then, like in your case, we add 'FE' if it's a girl!"

The doctor asked Alan if he wanted to cut the cord. "I think I'll let you do that," he said. Then they cleaned up our baby and handed her to me. My body started trembling uncontrollably.

Alan and I cried and held her, and thanked God that she was beautiful, with all her fingers and toes.

We named her Mattie Denise, in honor of Alan's mother and me. We were overwhelmed with joy and a strange, sweet surge of adrenaline, and we talked uncontrollably about everything that had happened. It was one of those rare times when everything else drops away completely, one of those moments when time seems to stop and you're at the still hub of life's big wheel.

Then the wheel started turning again. I stayed in the hospital for a day and a half. There was a radio in the room, and it seemed like Alan's song was playing every hour on the hour. I was overwhelmed. Alan's career was taking off in a big way, and more importantly, our beautiful baby daughter had arrived. It was as if all of our dreams were finally coming true, right before our eyes.

But that didn't last long.

Chapter 9

LIFE THROWS CURVES

∝⚹ᴑ

We lived and learned, life threw curves
There was joy, there was hurt
Remember when

Alan Jackson, "Remember When,"

Nothing made me happier than holding our tiny, precious baby girl and knowing that she was healthy and normal. I prided myself on the fact that I had rigorously watched my diet and made sure to get just the right amount of protein every day. We had learned in our childbirth classes that this was important for strong brain development. (Indeed, Mattie has proven herself to be an exceptionally intelligent girl over the years. Never mind the great genes she must have gotten from both her parents!)

But with this new joy came tremendous disappointment as I realized that Alan had to leave town the day before I'd go home from the hospital. While I was grateful that he had been present for the birth, and that I hadn't gone into labor while he was on the road, performing, I was also sad that he wouldn't be with me to bring our first baby home.

I had held a happy homecoming picture in my mind—both of us laughing and carrying our new baby into our little home, together—ever since we found out I was pregnant. Now it would just be me. And though I didn't really realize it at the time, a lot of the happy expectations I'd had about our dream-come-true life were, in fact, rather different from its reality.

Marty Gamblin's wonderful wife Cherie, who had been such a good friend to us over the years, offered to bring Mattie and me home. She helped us pack up everything, including many massive flower arrangements from Arista, record executives, and family and friends, and then joined a couple of nurses as they pushed the wheelchair holding me and Mattie outside to her minivan. There was no fanfare as there would have been if Alan had been with us. Even though he had had only two singles out by then, people were already recognizing him from his first CD cover.

I rode in the back with Mattie next to me in her new car seat. Even with the extra padding around her, she seemed so small and scrunched. I was just beginning to realize that as a new mother, I was going to worry about everything: Is she straight enough, is the sun in her eyes, is she cold, is she hot, is she wet, is she hungry? She made it home to our basement apartment in much better shape than I did.

Tears and Fears

As a teenager I'd never done babysitting, and as the youngest in our family, I hadn't helped to take care of little siblings. I realized—belatedly—that I knew just about nothing about the care and feeding of babies.

Cherie helped unload all the stuff that we had accumulated at the hospital. We had all kinds of pamphlets on child safety, choosing a doctor for your baby, tips on breastfeeding, post-partum depression, and a thousand other topics that I had never had reason to think about before, but that now seemed quite important.

All four of our parents had driven up from Georgia the day after Mattie was born. Alan's mother and daddy offered to stay with me until Alan returned from his trip that weekend. Alan's mother prepared meals and took care of our little house so I could tend to Mattie. I was like a nervous cat. I could not relax, even though Mattie seemed content to eat and sleep. I stood over her bassinet, watching her anxiously.

Stress and Sleepless Nights

At least the feeding part went well. Mattie took to breastfeeding right away, and by her two-week checkup she was thriving. But during the third week, I began to notice that she was crying more and more . . . particularly after she nursed. I made sure that she was burped adequately and that everything else was fine, but she would cry and pull her knees up to her little chest in a fetal position. It was clear that her stomach was hurting.

When I made a call to one of my friends with three daughters who had survived infancy (along with their mother), she informed me that Mattie had colic. In the months that followed,

I acquired a tremendous amount of advice, both solicited and unsolicited, on how to relieve colic. Mothers, grandmothers, professionals, and strangers who stopped me on the street all gave input about Mattie's condition, and I could have written a book. Oh, wait, I *am* writing a book. But not about colic. Never mind.

Unfortunately, nothing helped. By now all the relatives had returned to the peace of quiet Newnan. Alan was out of town, working at least four days of each week. It didn't take long for me to think that I had made a big mistake, or at least that I was the most incompetent mother in the world.

> IT DIDN'T TAKE LONG FOR ME TO THINK THAT I HAD MADE A BIG MISTAKE, OR AT LEAST THAT I WAS THE MOST INCOMPETENT MOTHER IN THE WORLD.

Alan was always a smart thinker and a good problem solver, but he would get so distressed that the baby was crying—and that he couldn't relieve her pain—that I felt like I needed to take her away, out of his hearing. It was almost a relief when he and his band would leave town on Thursdays.

As the weeks dragged on, we resorted to anything that might possibly help. We put Mattie on her stomach on top of the dryer while it was on, at the suggestion of a friend who had heard that the warm vibrations would soothe a colicky baby's stomach. It might have distracted her for a moment, but it was no solution. We even tried running the vacuum cleaner near her after someone told us that that had helped her infant. The vacuum helped our rugs, but not our baby.

The only temporary solution came from above. My friend and our upstairs landlord, Donna Thompson, would come down to our basement apartment after she arrived home from work. Donna was an angel in disguise: she would bring a hot meal; insist that I take a warm, relaxing bath; and take Mattie outside, far enough away so that I could not hear her crying. That short intermission from the howling did more for my soul than Donna will ever know.

One night we were invited to dinner at the home of country great George Jones; he and his wife, Nancy, had become wonderful friends. It was a lovely evening—except that Mattie cried the entire time. Alan made light of it, crediting it to the fact that the baby's infancy had thus far been spent in a basement apartment. "You'd cry too," he told George and Nancy, "if you were seeing light for the first time!"

Moving Up: Out of the Basement

When Mattie was two and a half months old, Alan's success was such that we could do something about our housing. We left the little basement apartment, with its calico curtains, old couch, dented mattress, and the brown shag carpeting. Now that we had some money, we could upgrade, so Alan located a beautiful brick home in the nicely landscaped, lovely neighborhood of Burton Hills in a very desirable area of town.

The house belonged to Crystal Gayle, and she rented it out

now and then. Our "yard sale" furniture would not look quite right in it, to say the least. "That's okay," Alan told me. "You just go and get stuff, whatever you want. We can afford it now."

We had not had the money to buy furniture or accessories before. I didn't really even know what I liked—or, more important, what Alan would like. He had always made every major purchase, and I had always been happy with what *he* wanted.

The very thought of taking Mattie to furniture stores while I browsed made me nervous. What if she cried incessantly? Would the store clerks think of me as a bad mother? I couldn't control Mattie's crying at home, so how was I going to be focused enough in a store to buy furniture? I began to feel more and more inadequate . . . and the longer I did nothing, the worse I felt.

Moving day arrived, and Alan was on the road. His parents came to help me, and we arrived at our new home to find that the workmen who had refinished the hardwood floors hadn't exactly finished in time. When I walked in, holding my screaming baby, the floors were still sticky with stain and gluey polyurethane.

It was a last-straw moment. My husband was out every night, singing to screaming women who were throwing their personal clothing onto the stage . . . and here I was, without him, and we couldn't even move into our home because it had glue-trap floors. I burst into tears.

If Alan had been with me, we would have probably laughed about it and come up with a solution as a team. Without him, the floor problem felt like yet another sticky wicket I had to pass through on my own . . . and another daunting reality that was so different from my happy expectations.

The floors eventually dried, and we moved in. Over the next few months, whenever Alan came home from the road, he was disappointed that I hadn't made much progress with furnishing the house. He wanted me to be able to enjoy the new life we had always wanted.

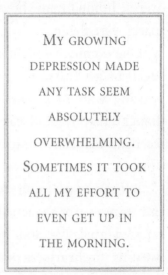

My depression made any task seem absolutely overwhelming. Sometimes it took all my effort to even get out of bed in the morning. Since our move, I had lost Donna's wonderful support, and Mattie was a huge challenge. And now Alan—ever so capable and confident—was hoping for me to take pleasure in our lovely but intimidating new life. I was so down on myself that even though he wasn't trying to control me, I felt like he would second-guess every choice I made, so I didn't make any choices at all.

MY GROWING DEPRESSION MADE ANY TASK SEEM ABSOLUTELY OVERWHELMING. SOMETIMES IT TOOK ALL MY EFFORT TO EVEN GET UP IN THE MORNING.

Alan did everything he could think of to lift me out of my dark valley. He took me on an idyllic trip to Hawaii, encouraged me to get whatever help I needed. He desperately wanted me to feel better.

"Nisey, you're going to be all right," he'd say. "You can have everything that you want now," he'd say. "We have a beautiful new baby, my career is going great . . . why can't you be happy?"

I asked myself the same questions. I felt like there had been too many changes too fast. Within a few months I had stopped working at the job I loved, had a baby, and moved into a big home that felt overwhelming. Alan was suddenly America's new country heartthrob and was gone at least four days a week. I was on a runaway train barreling down the tracks. I had no control over it, I didn't know how to stop it or even slow it down, and sparks were flying.

One evening we went out to eat at a local restaurant. Mattie began to get fussy, and some people around us were already noticing who Alan was. Rather than cause a disturbance, I thought that I could calm Mattie by nursing her under her receiving blanket. I draped it over my shoulder as I held her close.

But she began to scream even harder, flailing her little arms, and to my surprise, actually pushed the blanket off me. I was exposed—briefly—and humiliated for much longer. I was sweating, my heart was pounding, and I would have turned back time if I could. I just wanted my old life back, the life I knew, with Alan at home, free from demands I could not handle.

Buses, Buddies, and Bidets

Meanwhile, after four years of rejections and setbacks, Alan was finally living his music dream, big-time. He bought his first Silver Eagle tour bus with a loan from our newest best friend at SunTrust Bank, Brian Williams. Alan and his band rolled in style all over the country, opening for Loretta Lynn, Conway Twitty, George Jones, Merle Haggard, Alabama, the Judds, and other headliners.

During this time Alan played a big club one night to a sold-out crowd. His tour manager, Carson, told Alan that when he was finished, he should just exit stage left, go through the door there, and Carson would be waiting to escort him to the bus.

Alan played his show, finished his last song, and waved to the cheering crowd. Then he turned and walked off the stage to the right. He found the door, opened it, and strode confidently through, still exhilarated by the crowd's enthusiasm.

As he went over the threshold, he fell out of the doorway and into a pitch-black vacant lot outside. He had gone out the wrong door, and here he was, the big new star, stuck in waist-high weeds and trash outside the theater. It was so dark that he could not see a thing. He just stood there . . . and then within two or three minutes, he saw a flashlight beam bobbing through the weeds. It was his manager, coming to rescue him.

> AS HE WENT OVER THE THRESHOLD, HE FELL OUT OF THE DOORWAY AND INTO A PITCH-BLACK VACANT LOT OUTSIDE. HE HAD GONE OUT THE WRONG DOOR, AND HERE HE WAS, THE BIG NEW STAR, STUCK IN WAIST-HIGH WEEDS AND TRASH OUTSIDE THE THEATER.

"Alan!" Carson whispered. "Psssst! Alan! Over here!"

Soon Alan was in safer venues. His first yearlong tour had him opening for Randy Travis, who was selling out 20,000-seat arenas.

This was heady stuff. Other than the isolated and sometimes grimy bars where he had played in his lean years, Alan hadn't really been much of anywhere except Florida a few times, a big trip to Washington, D.C., when he was twelve, and family camping trips to Alabama.

Now he was traveling the country, lavished with attention. It was all so new. He still remembers staying at his first elegant hotel. He walked into the bathroom, and there was a strange device he'd never seen before. It was next to the toilet, a low, ceramic basin with faucets and spray. He knew it wasn't a water fountain. He knew it was in the bathroom for a reason. It was a bidet, of course, but Alan had never heard of such a thing.

Even if he didn't know what a bidet was back then, he was still a star. On tour, people could not get close to him unless they had an "all-access" pass. He was escorted everywhere, even in the secured areas, by his tour manager. Just hanging out with the crew and band at each venue was energizing. They'd do a sound check together in the afternoon, have a catered meal somewhere in the building, and then shower and relax on the bus until time for the show.

Afterward, they often had pizza and beer brought to the bus. They'd debrief on the particulars of the show as they headed off to the next city, laughing at funny things that had happened, from missed notes, forgotten lyrics, or other train wrecks, to crazy things that extreme fans would do.

When they went out to eat, one of the band members had the habit of getting into the restaurant first, ordering his food first, and expecting to get his order first so he could eat first. (Maybe he had issues about being a youngest child and had grown up hungry or something.) Alan would always quietly take the waiter aside, slip him some cash, and tell him to mess up this person's order or to bring it out long after everyone else had been served. The guy never could quite figure out why, for years on the road, he was always served last. (Eventually Alan told him what he'd been doing, and the band all had a big laugh.)

Aside from the camaraderie and acclaim on the road, Alan could also look forward to coming back to a real home done up in real style. This, too, was a reminder that he'd achieved his dreams, that his long-sought success and status were now a reality. All was well . . . at least as far as he was concerned.

Chapter 10

SPOTLIGHTS AND SHADOWS

I tried to stay on the straight and narrow
But I've walked a crooked path
and I've felt worthy of forgiveness
and deservin' heaven's wrath
Right on the money and off by a mile
Ahead of my time and way out of style

Harry Allen and Gary Cotton, "Life or Love"

Of course I was happy about Alan's career success. It was our dream come true. I laughed at his funny stories and was thrilled to hear his descriptions of packed arenas and cheering crowds.

But his retelling of the stories wasn't the same as living them. I had had lots of pictures in my mind of what success would look and feel like. And in all of them, I had envisioned that I'd be right by Alan's side, or at least cheering from backstage, while we enjoyed the new adventures of his musical career. Instead, I was lost, confused, and at home with a baby who would not stop crying.

In an attempt to make me feel better, Alan encouraged me to go get a new engagement ring. I couldn't help but feel how different things were now than in the early days of our relationship. Years ago he had carefully saved, plotted, chosen, wrapped, and surprised me with my first small ring . . . and now he wasn't able to even go with me to pick out a new one. We could afford a much bigger diamond—but the price was a lot less of my husband.

I invited my friend Ame to come from Newnan to Nashville for a ring-designing visit. She tried her best to make it fun and to add some excitement to our outing to the jewelers. I chose a gorgeous two-and-a-half-carat marquis diamond with triangular diamonds on each side. As proud as I was of my new ring, I would have given it—or anything else—to feel relieved of my melancholy.

Coming Out of the Blues

I knew about postpartum depression, but having a label for it didn't help. I was overwhelmed, with the feeling of a gray curtain draped over me. I could not just "get a grip" and feel better. I could go through the motions, but I could not imagine this dark fog ever lifting. What made it worse was that friends would tell me I had everything and should be the happiest woman in the world. Regardless of how I "should" feel, I felt alone, inadequate, and overwhelmed.

After confiding in a few close friends, I decided to see my doctor. He helped me deal with some of the anxiety and postpartum issues, and prescribed medication that eventually cleared the clouds of depression. With my brain chemistry in balance, I was finally able to deal with basic things like furniture, and I was able to enjoy some of the fruits of the success we had sought for so long. And, thankfully, Mattie's colic got better, and she became the cheerful, easygoing person she still is today.

> WITH RECORD ROYALTIES ROLLING IN, ALAN PLEADED WITH ME. "DENISE," HE SAID, "YOU KNOW YOU REALLY *CAN* QUIT YOUR JOB NOW!"

Newly energized and feeling stronger, I was able to interview and hire housekeeping help and a nanny. For the first time in our lives, we weren't watching every penny. We bought furniture. Fun clothes. Cars. And after taking repeated leaves of absence from my flight-attendant position at US Air, I was finally able to let it go. I had held on to that job like it was a security blanket, thinking that if Alan's success and all our new money suddenly evaporated, I could always return to flying. But with record royalties rolling in, Alan pleaded with me. "Denise," he said, "you know you really *can* quit your job now!"

Good Enough?

We stayed in Crystal Gayle's rental home until we found the house we wanted to buy: a historic Revolutionary War–era farmhouse with ten acres around it and pastures for horses.

Renovating, furnishing, and decorating it took a lot of time and focus.

By this time Mattie was toddling around and talking a little. Alan bought me my first full-length fur coat. I put it on, twirling for our little daughter. Mattie reached up to me, petted the thick, smooth fur, and shouted, "Doggie! Doggie!"

Soon after that we were in Washington, D.C. President George H. W. Bush loved country music, and Alan was asked to perform at the historic Ford's Theatre for the president. Afterward, at the White House, I smiled and shook hands with George and Barbara Bush. I felt like I was having an out-of-body experience, seeing the scene and thinking, *How can this be real? How can all this be happening to us?*

The White House was one thing. Life on the road was a little more raw. By this point Alan had been in *People* magazine's "25 Most Beautiful People" issue; he was Nashville's "Best New Male Artist," "Star of Tomorrow," winner of "Album of the Year," and country music's latest sex symbol. *Here in the Real World*, with sales over one million, had gone platinum. The attention was intense. At concerts and events, women reacted to Alan like he was Elvis. The media scrutiny was ever-present. You never knew when you'd turn around and a photographer would be in your face. The challenge was to look good, all the time.

All this "worldly" focus on image and appearance was superficial, sure . . . but I didn't have any other deep concept of real significance and identity that could counter it. The Christian faith I'd grown up with wasn't really a part of my everyday life, so it wasn't the basis of my self-image. I was caught up in the illusions of a *People*-magazine world that worships at the altar of celebrity, beauty, wealth, and fame.

The Gospel had told me the truth that I was special and significant simply because I was a child of God, not because of how I looked or how many good things I'd done. The songs of my youth had told me that "Jesus loves me, this I know, 'cause the Bible tells me so." I knew that Jesus loved me "just as I am," as the old hymn put it. And I had sung more times than I could count:

> Turn your eyes upon Jesus,
> Look full in His wonderful face;
> And the things of earth will grow strangely dim
> In the light of His glory and grace.

But now I wasn't turning my eyes upon Jesus. He seemed far away and irrelevant, the soft-eyed Savior whose portrait hung on the wall of my church fellowship hall back home. And the things of earth were not "strangely dim." They were as clear and sharp as the glossy magazines with Alan's picture on the cover and maybe a shot of me inside, on the red carpet at the Country Music Awards, wearing some sparkly designer gown.

I wasn't clinically depressed anymore, but the pressures of celebrity compounded bleak feelings I'd had since I was a teenager. "Do I look good enough?" "What are they thinking about me?" "Am I thin enough?"

But now the stakes were much higher: we weren't in little Newnan, Georgia, anymore, where I was cheerleading captain and a big fish in a tiny pond. We were out in the big leagues, the "real world," though it didn't feel quite real at all. People were building us up, polishing the shiny glow of Alan's celebrity. Money was pouring in. These were big, seductive, confusing forces at work in our world . . . and I was finding that my teenage-sized faith just wasn't strong enough to counter them.

DELIGHTS AND DISTRACTIONS

❧

If you want to drive a big limousine
I'll buy the longest one you've ever seen
I'll buy you tall, tall trees
And all the waters in the seas
I'm a fool, fool, fool for you
If you want to own a great big mansion
Well I'll give it my utmost attention
I'll buy you tall, tall trees
And all the waters in the seas

George Jones and Roger Miller, "Tall, Tall Trees"

I buried any feelings of concern or insecurity under the benefits of Alan's success. I now had the time and money to get my nails and hair done regularly, to get facials and other spa services as I wished, and to shop and enjoy being with girlfriends. I enjoyed the new role of being the "star wife" and getting tons of attention from fans.

Alan had bought a boat that we enjoyed taking to Center Hill Lake, a beautiful deepwater lake about an hour and a half away. It had a lovely enclosed cabin for Mattie to take naps and get out of the sun. Alan made sure I always had a new Cadillac to drive. No need to work or worry. We had no material needs at all—just more and more luxuries.

One of the high points in Alan's early career was his induction as a member of the Grand Ole Opry. We invited our parents to come up from Georgia to share the occasion with us. Alan was performing on the show that evening and had to go early for some media interviews. I decided to take our parents out to dinner before we headed to the Opry House.

We headed off to a local catfish restaurant that I knew they'd all enjoy. It was unusually busy that night. I soon realized that we were going to be late to the Opry, so when we finally got our food, I made everyone wolf it down. The problem was, my mother is just not a wolfer. I told her, quite respectfully, to either put her fried fish fillet down, or bring it with her, because we had to leave.

"Mother," I said, "I have waited a very long time for this night, and I am *not* going to miss it!"

We left the restaurant, still chewing, and I have never driven so fast in all my life. We flew down the interstate toward the Opry House, whizzing past all the other cars as little Mattie looked out the window, babbling "bye-bye!" to each one. Later, Alan's daddy had a plaque made for me, commemorating my race-car driving and suggesting that I enter the next Indy 500.

But we made it on time to the Opry.

Dick Clark's Unanswered Prayer

When Alan was nominated for his first Academy of Country Music Award, we were thrilled. We flew to L.A. for this big Dick Clark production, one of our first live television award shows. As you know, these award shows are very tightly controlled in terms of time. Every award winner is cautioned to keep acceptance speeches short and to the point so the show can keep on schedule with its commercial breaks.

Well, to Alan's absolute surprise, he won the award for Best New Artist. He walked up onstage, his heart overflowing with joy and wonder, and commenced thanking every single person he could think of. He thanked everyone at the record label and the publishing company. He expressed his deep gratitude to me and our parents. He thanked his sec-

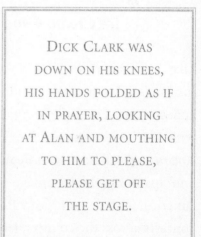

DICK CLARK WAS DOWN ON HIS KNEES, HIS HANDS FOLDED AS IF IN PRAYER, LOOKING AT ALAN AND MOUTHING TO HIM TO PLEASE, PLEASE GET OFF THE STAGE.

ond cousins, aunts, uncles, neighbors, and third-grade teacher. He went on and on. He didn't want to miss anybody, and he wanted to make sure that if he never, ever won another award, at least he had already expressed his appreciation to everyone who had anything to do with his music career.

First the teleprompter message came on. "Wrap it up!" it said politely. Alan saw it but kept going.

Then the band started to play to encourage him to stop. Alan kept talking, making himself heard over it.

Finally he looked over to the side of the theater curtains, just offstage, and saw Dick Clark. Dick was down on his knees, his hands folded as if in prayer, looking at Alan and mouthing to him to *please, please get off the stage.*

Dick's prayer was not answered. Alan kept on thanking people, and finally the awards show just cut to a commercial.

Ice Cream Cones and Puppy Dogs

Like his first record, Alan's second album, *Don't Rock the Jukebox*, sold more than a million copies and went platinum. He appeared on *The Tonight Show* with Jay Leno, *The Late Show* with David Letterman, *The Today Show*, and *Good Morning America*. He chatted with Regis and Kathy Lee, sang for Oprah, and his long, lanky image filled television screens across America. Jetting from Nashville to New York to L.A., and playing concerts across the country, left him little time to be at home.

When he was home, he wanted to spend as much time with Mattie as possible. One day, when she was a toddler, he told me to get some rest. "Nisey, you take a nap, okay, and I'll just take Mattie out for some ice cream." That was especially kind of him, since I was pregnant again and feeling quite tired.

I lay down on our bed, so grateful that my sensitive husband understood how much I needed rest. *He is so understanding,* I thought as I drowsed off into dreamland. *So thoughtful.*

I woke to a different thought. Mattie burst into our bedroom, her hands sticky from ice cream, screaming at the top of her small lungs.

"Mommy!" she yelled. "Daddy got me ice cream! And a puppy! His name is Buddy!"

The next thing I knew, a tiny black-and-white dog of unknown parentage was barking, running in circles around our bedroom, and trying to jump up on the bed. His snout was covered with ice cream, and Alan was grinning so much that I realized that even though I didn't want all the work of taking care of a new puppy, I had no choice. This dog was now a family member. (Fourteen years later, Buddy is still the alpha dog at the Jackson home; he's even the mascot for Alan's record label.)

Around the same time we decided that a secluded lake house would be a perfect getaway from our frantic lifestyle, and we wanted our children to grow up with the same great memories of boating and skiing that Alan had growing up. By this point Mattie had grown into a sweet, happy toddler. She was very cooperative and eager to please, and Alan and I were both thrilled about being pregnant with our second child.

Wait, Baby, Wait

This pregnancy was a lot like my first, and again, to the chagrin of my female friends, I wasn't sick at all, having a very easy time of it until the day my labor pains started. I knew from my birthing classes that the earlier in the labor process that you go to the hospital, the higher your chances for a C-section. I again wanted to have the baby naturally, and since walking brings on labor, I started strolling around the house.

I walked in circles, walking, walking, trying to move the labor along so we could go to the hospital. Mattie trotted along next to me, excited about the new baby on the way, though she had no precise idea of exactly how the baby would come out of Mommy and into the world. Neither did I, really. I walked until the labor pains became so intense that I knew the time was short. I called the doctor.

> ON THE WAY TO THE HOSPITAL I STARTED TO PANIC. *I AM GOING TO HAVE THIS BABY RIGHT HERE IN THIS CAR,* I THOUGHT. *AND ALAN IS GOING TO HAVE TO DELIVER IT, AND WE'RE GOING TO BE ON THE COVER OF EVERY STAR MAGAZINE IN AMERICA . . .*

It was a lovely summer day. Alan was outside, ready to take me to the hospital, of course, but preoccupied with some kind of car deal. He loved buying, selling, trading, and fixing vehicles, and he was bartering with somebody about a truck.

I called for Alan.

"Okay, I'm coming!" he shouted back.

I grabbed my hospital bag. I felt like things were moving along pretty quickly now. "Alan!" I shouted. "We've got to *go!*"

"I'm coming!" he yelled. He flew into the house, finally abandoning his truck deal, took a look at me, and hustled me into the car. On the way to the hospital I started to panic. *I am going to have this baby right here in this car,* I thought. *And Alan is going to have to deliver it, and we're going to be on the cover of every star magazine in America. . .*

We careened into the hospital. The nurses were calm but clear about the urgency of the situation once they checked me. "This baby's about to crown," one said. "Let's get the doctor."

He arrived from his office next door and barely had enough time to wash his hands before Alexandra Jane Jackson arrived. (She's named Jane in honor of my sister.) She was strong, beautiful, and healthy, and we overflowed with gratitude to God.

Alan's song "Chattahoochee" had hit the top of the charts just before Ali was born, and Arista had already planned a big #1 party for Alan the evening after her birth. Alan sent the head of his video crew to film a greeting from me to be played at the festivities. I held our new baby in my arms and smiled into the camera. "Alan has achieved many accomplishments over the past few years," I said, "and I'm holding one of his very greatest ones right here in my arms." Someone who was at the party told me later that Alan had a hard time holding back his tears.

As the weeks went by, Ali developed colic, but the fussiness and discomfort passed within a few weeks. My coping skills were much better the second time around.

"Chattahoochee" stayed at #1 for a month, and its album eventually sold more than six million copies. Then Alan's first Christmas album was released in October. Our lake house was completed, and we celebrated Thanksgiving there, holding our new baby, playing with Mattie, and looking out over the clear blue waters. We had much to be thankful for.

Return of the T-Bird

The Christmas after Ali was born, I surprised Alan with a gift that I'll never be able to surpass. With the help of one of Alan's friends, Doug Channell, and a lot of detective work, I was able to track down the 1955 Thunderbird convertible that had been Alan's first love. The very same car we had dated in, the car that represented countless hours of Alan's youth . . . It belonged to a pilot in North Carolina, and he was willing to sell it. I won't tell you how much it cost me.

The car was delivered to Nashville, and we hid it in the garage of our friend and business manager, Debbie Doebler. On Christmas morning, a light snow was falling, and we opened all our presents. Mattie was happily playing with her new toys, and the baby was sleepy . . . but then I couldn't stand it anymore.

"Alan," I said, "I have one more present for you, but we have to go over to Debbie Doebler's to get it."

He didn't want to take the little girls out in the snow, but I insisted. We piled into the car. As we pulled into Debbie's driveway, I pushed the remote door opener I'd brought along, and Debbie's garage door slowly lifted. Alan knew something was up, of course, and as soon as he saw the front grill of the car, he started to smile.

"You bought a Thunderbird just like my first car!" he said.

"No," I said. "Alan, that *is* your car!"

I have never seen Alan Jackson so surprised. He just sat there, tears in his eyes, and then he jumped out of my car and into the Thunderbird, rubbing the seats, checking the gauges, thinking of the hours he and his daddy had spent making that car so special.

He opened the trunk, and there was the 1955 license tag that he'd painted as a teenager. He was beside himself.

Later, as I drove the girls back home, I kept looking in my rearview mirror . . . and there was Alan, following in his convertible, grinning ear to ear and looking like an adolescent boy.

But then, just a few months later, the day before my thirty-fourth birthday, came the tragedy I could never have imagined back when we were teenagers . . . or ever, for that matter.

Chapter 12

TURNING MY EYES

❦

I'm lost in the night
The icy wind is howling out your name
And desolation lingers
Like a fog
The fire is growing dimmer
In the wind

I'm out in the rain
The moon has gone behind the cloud again
And I can't stand to live
Another day
'Cause my bluebird went away

Leon Russell, "Bluebird"

Alan and I had gone to our lake house for an evening alone to celebrate my birthday. Our nanny, Mary Miller, was going to bring Mattie and Ali up the next morning for them to celebrate with us and spend a few days at our new retreat. It was late afternoon; I was sipping iced tea and reading a book on the chaise longue in our spacious mint-green bedroom. I looked up as Alan came in, and his face was white.

My first thought was that my daddy had died. He was eighty years old, and I'd been steeling myself for the day he would pass on.

But I had not prepared myself for what came next.

Alan sat down beside me. "Nisey," he said slowly, "something terrible has happened to your older brother."

I held my breath.

"Nisey," he said again, "Ronald has killed himself."

I couldn't believe what I was hearing. Ron had been the rock of stability in our family. He was two decades older than me; I had looked up to him all my life as my "young daddy." While I had watched my twin brother, Danny, struggle with all kinds of uncertainty and unhealthy choices, Ron had seemed so stable and secure.

My Big Brother

After graduating from college, he had built a beautiful home on an unspoiled lake in a very desirable neighborhood. He had worked in management for the same company for thirty years and had a happy family life with grown sons. He was a responsible, hardworking man with high morals and Christian values. I couldn't believe that my older brother, my hero, had somehow been in so much emotional pain that he could have taken his own life.

Gradually, though, we found out the parts of Ron's story that we had not known. Like many of us, he had seemed fine on the surface, but was struggling with issues deep inside.

We had known that Ron's company had gone through a reorganization that forced early retirement for many of its high management employees, including my brother. We didn't know how much the loss of his long-term position and role shook him, however. He didn't know what to do, or who would employ him at the level to which he was accustomed, at age fifty-five.

We had offered Ron the opportunity to temporarily move to Tennessee and head a restaurant business we were considering. He could do that, we thought, while he figured out his next career step. He stayed at our lake house while he looked for a restaurant site in the area.

Meanwhile, my father had been going through some difficult times of his own, and Ron took my dad's struggles to heart more than we realized. My daddy began to show all the classic symptoms of bipolar disorder, with bizarre and uncharacteristic behaviors. He began exhibiting classic signs of mania: he could not sleep, had to have his way, and engaged in all sorts of wild, excessive activities. He decided he was going to set the Coweta County government straight in Newnan; then he was going to fix the state system; and then he was single-handedly going to revamp the entire United States federal government. He'd stay up late at night, typing papers and plans, then call people non-stop, talking fast.

We think now that Daddy probably had a mild stroke that affected his brain . . . but at the time, Ron was evidently worried that he'd end up just like our father, though Ron was more depressed than manic.

When he had no real luck with finding restaurant property for us in Tennessee, we suggested that he return to Newnan. We decided to put the restaurant idea on hold for a while, not knowing how that would compound his anxiety about his future. Soon after Ron returned home from Tennnesse, he would wait for Debby to leave for work and then go to my parent's house wearing his bedroom slippers, unshaven, and ungroomed. He'd lie on my Mother's couch and sleep for hours, returning home later in the afternoon. Although this behavior was certainly out of character for him, my parents thought that he was merely tired . . . no one could see the depth of his despair.

Ron eventually told his wife, Debby, how awful he was feeling. Although he told her he was having suicidal thoughts, he also assured her that he would never hurt her or his family by acting on his thoughts. Debby immediately took my brother to a psychiatrist who put him on Zoloft but didn't insist that he be hospitalized. As a precautionary measure, Debby and their boys removed all the hunting guns from their home. Then Debby and Ron told me, Alan, and my sister Jane about his deep depression. Because my parents were dealing with my father's maniac behavior, we all decided not to burden them with the news of my brother's depression.

Fourteen days after starting his medication, my brother found a gun. He wrote a note to Debby, walked down to the lake...the same lake where he had taught his three boys to fish and where we had all had so many good times together...and ended his horrible pain. Part of the note he left Debby read, "I don't want to become like Daddy." Sadly, we learned later that the most critical time during the treatment of depression is two to three weeks after starting antidepressants. Around this time, the depressed person sometimes finds that he has enough new energy to actually act on his suicidal thoughts but does not have enough medicine in his system to really feel better.

Sobbing over Ron's awful choice, I remembered his last phone call. It had been just a few days earlier, and I'd told him that things were going to be just fine. Now I realized that he had called me to say good-bye.

My brother's death made me begin to think about my spirituality for the first time in many years. I began to think about life after death, and how some people believed that suicides couldn't go to heaven. But I also knew in my heart that the loving God I knew would never take away Ron's salvation because of a choice he had made in desperation. I thought about eternal life . . . and deliverance from sin . . . and loss.

> I HAD ALWAYS FELT STRONGLY ABOUT THE IMPORTANCE OF RAISING MY CHILDREN IN THE CHURCH . . . AND NOW HERE I WAS, SO HAPPY AND BUSY WITH OUR HOUSES, CARS, PLANES, AND TOYS THAT I HADN'T EVEN THOUGHT ABOUT CHURCH—OR MORE IMPORTANTLY, OUR SPIRITUAL LIVES—IN A VERY LONG TIME.

I also began to admit to myself that our children weren't growing up with a real spiritual perspective. Ali was only eight months old, but Mattie was almost four. She needed to be in Sunday school. I had always felt strongly about the importance of raising my children in the church . . . and now here I was, so happy and busy with our houses, cars, planes, and toys that I hadn't even thought about church—or more importantly, our spiritual lives—in a very long time.

My brother's awful death, however, stopped me cold. What was life really about? Could strength and comfort come from God . . . or was that just nice Sunday school talk that couldn't really apply to the hard challenges of real life?

Those kinds of questions were too disturbing. I didn't know how to answer them. I just wanted to feel better. So I managed to submerge hard thoughts under the fast-running stream of our lives. They would pop up again later, like beach balls that you just can't hold under water . . . but for the time being I focused on more superficial things.

Drifting on a Pretty River

At the end of that year, for our fifteenth anniversary, Alan surprised me even more than he had before with the engagement ring on the night he proposed when we were young. This time it was not a small diamond, however. This was a five-and-a-half-carat emerald-cut diamond with forty smaller diamonds set in a wide yellow-gold band. It reached my knuckle and threw sparkled rainbows in the sunshine. If Alan had surprised me as an eighteen-year-old, now I found myself constantly amazed by his ability to make every situation seem perfect.

A week later, on Christmas morning, he led me out to one of the garages . . . and there was a gleaming black Mercedes convertible with a huge red bow around it. Next to it was a shiny miniature version of the same car with a matching bow . . . for the girls.

These lovely material things distracted me from the unseen beach-ball issues. I continued to push down anything in my consciousness that was painful or unpleasant, and skimmed along on the surface of my life, smiling lightly. Everything seemed perfect to outside observers. And while many things *were* good, all was not well in my inner core. I was drifting, without an anchor.

This didn't just affect *me*, of course. Since I had no real moorings, I was more dependent than ever on Alan's strength. His force of personality carried our marriage. We weren't two people pulling together, eyes ahead on the same goal, complementing each other's differences and strengthening each other.

Instead, my eyes were on Alan. Even though I had been more interested in a renewed relationship with God since Ron's suicide, I was still dependent—or I should say *codependent*—on Alan.

As the years went by, he'd bring it up now and then. He felt like we'd married so young and our relationship wasn't mature. He felt that I wasn't an equal partner, that I was too needy and relied on him too much. Deep down, I knew he was right. I couldn't have identified it at the time, but I feared not having his approval, just as I had so longed for my father's approval when I was a teenager.

Alan's personality didn't help my struggles. He wasn't shy about criticism. "Why do you have to always dress up when we go places?" he'd say. "Can't you just put on a flannel shirt and a baseball cap?"

Well, I didn't really like flannel shirts and baseball caps, but

I didn't know that. I didn't know what I liked or didn't like. All I knew was what Alan liked!

So I'd put on a baseball cap and a big plaid shirt just to please him. I don't know if he was intentionally trying to be controlling, or if his desire for me to look different was really about me *acting* different and being less dependent. I resented his control at the same time that I'd bend over backward to comply with it.

At any rate, every once in a while, one-sided discussions would surface in our marriage. For my part, I'd affirm that everything was just fine, go into an ostrich head-in-the-sand denial mode, and on we'd go. As long as everything looked good on the outside, I hid from myself the fact that things weren't so perfect on the inside.

Hair Bows and Letting Go

Even with the children, I cared too much what image they were presenting to the world. I made sure that our little girls had their matching outfits and big bows and little smocked dresses that seemed to be the expected norm within our circle of friends. Everyone looked at us as the "star's family," seeing if we were coiffed and dressed in the latest fashion. Subconsciously, I think I wanted people to look at Mattie and think, *Oh, look, Mattie's perfect, just like Denise, and Denise is such a good mother!*

Mattie was not particularly helpful with this little illusion. She hated ribbons and frills. She'd grab hold of the cute bow in her shiny hair, throw it down on the ground, and be happy as could be. Just like me when I was little—as my daddy had reminded me so often over the years—she wanted to be a boy. She had a boy's bowl haircut, and only wanted to wear boy tennis shoes, jeans, and baggy shirts. She did not want dolls. She did not want tiny monogrammed purses. If I tried to accessorize her, she'd sneak away and take off the cute little pink outfits and put on boyish clothes that didn't match.

At the time, I was so insecure that I thought people would see mismatched Mattie and think I was a bad mother. Now, though, whenever I see a child wearing strange clothes that don't go together, I don't think that she has a bad mother. No, I think she's got a mother with a healthy enough sense of self-confidence that she can let the child dress herself—she's not hyper-concerned about what other people might think.

A Circle of Friends

In fall 1995, Mattie started kindergarten at a private school in Nashville. I was glad to connect with other women who had children Mattie's age. One of them, Jane Smith, sent out an invitation to all the moms of the lower school students, inviting us to be a part of a prayer group in her home. I thought that being a part of this group would be a great way to make new friends, so I joined.

Not only did I form some great, long-lasting friendships, but my time spent with these women was the beginning of my real spiritual growth. We studied Christian parenting books. We confided our concerns for each of our children and prayed for God's blessings and protection for them.

Since I hadn't yet found a church home, Jane invited me to

visit hers. We started attending regularly. Mattie had school friends in her Sunday school class, so she enjoyed it. I also found a Sunday school class with a very gifted teacher, Robert Wolgemuth. I was drawn to the Scripture like never before. For the first time in my life, the Bible came alive for me. It was relevant. Personal. True. I began to look forward to Sunday mornings. The Gospel was presented in a way that I could apply it to my everyday life. Finally, my spiritual life was beginning to get back on track.

Dream Home

By this time, we had found a 140-acre horse farm on one of the most beautiful roads in Tennessee. The property itself wasn't par-

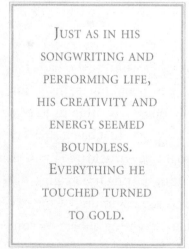

JUST AS IN HIS SONGWRITING AND PERFORMING LIFE, HIS CREATIVITY AND ENERGY SEEMED BOUNDLESS. EVERYTHING HE TOUCHED TURNED TO GOLD.

ticularly scenic, though, since it was rimmed by rusty, barbed-wire fences, and the pastures were full of weeds, sickly trees, and lots of manure. Eighteen years' worth of sawdust from the barn had been dumped beside the gentle river that wound past the acreage. It was a mess.

But Alan could see past all that to our new, long-term home. We bought it. It took a year just to clean it up, a year when Alan would walk the property every day he was in town, dreaming about its potential.

We built a quaint log cabin at the back of our land, overlooking the Harpeth River, and a red-roofed barn with a large apartment upstairs for guests. Then we built Alan's nineteen-car garage, an enclosed tennis court and basketball gym, and our gleaming white mansion with its curving stairways, breezy porches, and golden ceilings. An elaborate playhouse for the girls was outfitted far better than the houses in which Alan and I grew up. We put in lakes, outdoor fireplaces, gazebos, a white-sand beach, bridges, and waterfalls. There was a two-mile dirt racetrack for dune buggies and a grass runway for Alan's little red plane that he liked to fly now and then. The only thing we could not outbuild on the property was a *natural* wonder: a massive five-hundred-year-old oak tree, its roots sunk deep into the rich soil next to the winding river.

We called our estate "Sweetbriar." And as our enormous, stately home took shape, we met with designers to choose furniture, fabrics, custom chandeliers, intricate Italian tile, and exquisite carpentry for its interiors. Alan had a vision for every detail, down to the exact shade of gilt paint in the vaulted ceilings. Just as in his songwriting and performing life, his creativity and energy seemed boundless. Everything he touched turned to gold.

Baby Number Three

We moved in to our new home just six weeks before our third baby was due. Her nursery was fit for a princess. Mattie and Ali had waited eagerly for her arrival, not understanding why we couldn't just go to the hospital and get their baby sister out of Mommy's tummy. Once I did go into labor, Alan and I didn't waste any time before we headed to the hospital, remembering that we had almost waited too late with Ali. Still, we were at the hospital less than two hours before Dani Grace was born. (She was named Dani in honor of my daddy and my twin brother.) She was so beautiful, a perfect blessing. Surprisingly, she was exactly the same birth weight and height as Mattie had been.

Out of concern for our privacy, the hospital had decided to put up a temporary wall at the end of our hall so that no one could find our VIP birthing suite or our new baby. It amazed me how much everything had changed since Mattie's birth seven years earlier. The hospital was not going to take a chance that we would have any uninvited visitors. In fact, they posted a security guard by the temporary "wall" with a list of people we were expecting, and only those on the list were escorted back to our hidden suite. We were treated like royalty, not just at the hospital, but wherever we went. I had a fairy-tale life with my celebrity husband and my three beautiful daughters—one that I could not have imagined back when I was a young girl in Newnan, Georgia.

But then, when Dani was only three months old, a new surprise came from Alan. This surprise was not as welcome as the many he had given me over the long course of our marriage: he told me he was moving out.

Chapter 13

WHEN DREAMS DIE

Where did we go wrong
I wish I knew
It haunts me all the time
Now wherever I go and
Whatever I do
You're always on my mind

So tonight if you turn your radio on
You might hear a sad, sad song
About someone who lost everything they had
It may sound like me
But I'm a little bluer than that

Mark Irwin and Irene Kelley,
"A Little Bluer Than That"

stared at Alan. We were sitting in our huge bedroom suite beside the fireplace.

"Denise, I just can't go on like this," he said. "I just don't know how we can make it right. I'm not sure our relationship will ever be what it should be. That's not fair to either of us."

He was saying some of the same things he'd brought up periodically over the course of our marriage. He wasn't happy. We had married so young; were we really the best for each other? Or were we just stuck in a rut that we didn't know how to get out of? But then he added something he'd never said before.

"We need to separate. I'll be here for Christmas, for the girls, and then I'm going to the lake."

My stomach flipped. He was serious enough about this to move out of our home, away from our children.

It was right before Thanksgiving, 1997. Alan and I had been married almost eighteen years. We had come through so much together. We had three beautiful daughters. Mattie was seven, and Ali was four; Dani was just three months old.

Dani would smile a big baby smile when I smiled at her. But I couldn't smile much. Mostly I just cried. What should have been the happiest time in my life had become a bad dream. I was so angry and hurt that I could not really talk to Alan, except in the shortest sentences possible to make plans about the girls.

Relentless Pain

We somehow made it through Thanksgiving and Christmas. It was a terrible strain. We went through the motions of acting normal for the kids. During the holidays one of my girlfriends, trying to help, suggested that we get a group of friends together and take off for Steamboat Springs, Colorado.

Steamboat was snow-covered, beautiful . . . and absolutely desolate for me. My friends were wonderful, but all I could think about was Alan's looming departure.

As we were heading home and the plane barreled down the runway in Steamboat Springs, there was a huge rumble and thud. Maybe it was an engine misfiring. All I knew was that I'd never heard anything like it in all my years of flying, and we were just about to take off, the most critical time in the flight. I thought that the plane was going to crash.

Oddly enough, though, I didn't feel any fear at all. All I could think was that at least death would release me from this terrible emotional pain. For the first time in my life, I could begin to understand a little of what my brother Ron may have felt like before he took his own life. I wasn't suicidal—I knew I could not leave our children—but I felt absolutely overwhelmed by desperation and misery. I could understand how people can become dependent on alcohol or drugs. Anything to relieve the relentless pain.

Our flight from Steamboat made it into the air, and we arrived safely back in Nashville. I slowly climbed the curving staircase to our master bedroom suite and put my suitcase

> I SLOWLY CLIMBED THE CURVING STAIRCASE TO OUR MASTER BEDROOM SUITE AND PUT MY SUITCASE DOWN. MOST OF ALAN'S THINGS WERE GONE. I CRAWLED BETWEEN THE COOL, CRISP SHEETS IN OUR QUEEN-SIZED BED. ALONE.

down. Most of Alan's things were gone. I crawled between the cool, crisp sheets in our queen-sized bed. Alone.

Alan came back the next day . . . but only to retrieve a few clothes and to visit with the girls. And then I watched the only man I'd ever loved drive down the long road that led out of our dream home, away from the life we'd built together.

Alan soon realized that the lake house was too far away for him to visit regularly with the girls, so he rented a house close to the kids' school. He'd pick them up and take them out for ice cream, a movie, the park. As always, when he wasn't out of town, he wanted to be with the girls as much as possible. Both of us wanted to keep our emotions at bay and make life seem "normal." Whatever that was.

When we told Mattie and Ali that Daddy was going to live somewhere else, Mattie shook her head back and forth, tears on her round cheeks.

"But nothing's wrong!" she cried. "Why? Why?"

That was my question too. No marriage was perfect. Why did he expect so much? Why could he not just be happy with the way things were?

I also realized that I had known, down deep, Alan was right. Our relationship wasn't all it could be. But I hadn't wanted to face that fact, and so I'd buried it inside me somewhere. Now I thought back over our years together. Where did we go wrong?

Certainly the celebrity lifestyle had had its challenges, but we had weathered them pretty well. Alan was on the road a lot, and it always surprised me how some women threw themselves at him. Some enamored fans would go to any extreme to get his attention. I couldn't believe how aggressive they were. I'd tease him about it. "Baby, I don't remember women reacting to you like that when you were working second shift at the Newnan Kmart."

He'd just laugh. But he had to admit that all the attention made him feel good. His job was not unlike any other traveling job—there are always temptations, no matter who you are. When I had taken my flight attendant job, our families had wondered about the same issues for me.

The Quest to Feel Special

But regarding Alan, the swirls of rumors, innuendo, and viable concerns disturbed me. He had had a life on the road, and I wasn't part of it. We had agreed that my being home with our girls would help create a more "normal" childhood for them. Although that was wonderful, it wasn't always tremendously stimulating. Like many stay-at-home mothers, many nights I'd think back over the hours and wonder, *What did I really accomplish today?*

I had done important things, for sure: pushing one little daughter on a swing, helping another with an art project, fixing dinner, calling a friend who'd lost her dad. But people in the world aren't particularly impressed with such seemingly small accomplishments, and sometimes I felt that I didn't have a whole lot of purpose or worth in other people's eyes. I didn't have some product or creation or tangible accomplishment to show for my time.

Meanwhile, Alan was growing professionally, constantly making new music, thriving in his songwriting and singing life,

> LIFE REVOLVED AROUND WHAT ALAN DID—NOT BECAUSE THAT'S WHAT HE WANTED, BUT BECAUSE THAT'S WHAT I WANTED. IF SOMEONE HAD ASKED ME MY FAVORITE FOOD, OR MUSIC, OR MOVIE, I WOULDN'T HAVE KNOWN. BUT I KNEW ALAN'S.

striving toward new creative goals. He'd been releasing albums and receiving awards, recognition, and plenty of praise in his music, as well as getting all kinds of personal attention in the celebrity spotlight.

If Alan was growing in his work and getting plenty of personal affirmation, I felt like I was shrinking. After all, most of my identity was rooted in pretty superficial things: how I looked and what people thought of me—or what I thought they thought of me. I didn't have the deep roots of security that come from knowing real significance in a personal relationship with God.

And as I'd drifted from faith over the years, the only anchor in my life was Alan. Tethered to him, I had a sense of who I was. By his side, I was a woman to be envied. Life revolved around what Alan did—not because that's what he wanted, but because that's what I wanted. If someone had asked me my favorite food, or music, or movie, I wouldn't have known. But I knew Alan's.

Over the years, he had become my foundation. So when he left, there was nothing left for me to depend on. My house had been built on shifting sands, and now in the storms of fear, anger, pain, and confusion, I felt like everything was going to collapse.

Another awful thing about the break in our marriage was

that it wasn't just our private problem. It was public. Tabloids ran all kinds of painful headlines; reporters we'd never met speculated on our most personal thoughts. Ironically, I'd just been featured in a book that profiled "intimate interviews with the wives of today's hottest country superstars." I had to catch the publication before it came out and write an addendum to the chapter that profiled our story. There was a new chapter to our chapter, so to speak.

"Until this point in my life," I wrote, "I have had no major crises of any kind other than the sudden death of my brother Ron. This separation [has been] the most devastating experience I have ever gone through." I went on to write that I just couldn't imagine being faced with the possibility of being divorced from the only man I had ever loved—the man I had been with for more than two decades.

Alan was in pain too. His stomach was in a knot, and he lost twenty-five pounds in a few weeks. But he didn't want to settle anymore for an uneven partnership. I had become so needy and dependent, and he wanted something more. He wanted a woman who would be an equal partner, someone he could respect and admire.

I'm not saying that the break in our marriage was all about *my* shortfalls. Alan is the first to admit that he made bad choices. He had come to a point in his life, too, where he was realizing that all the material things in the world did not buy happiness. Everyone knows that . . . but it's another thing altogether to experience it. Alan had realized his greatest goals of music success, stardom, and enormous wealth and fame. But it didn't fill his heart.

One day he stood in front of our 25,000-square-foot mansion, looking over the perfect house and the perfectly manicured grounds and the perfect garages full of cars and boats and airplanes . . . and he whispered, "I'm still not happy."

In some ways I became the focal point of Alan's unhappiness. If all the long-sought pleasures of career success, stardom, and wealth weren't making him happy, then it must be the deficits in his marriage that were the root cause of his dissatisfaction.

But it's not up to me to analyze Alan's mind-set back then—or even now. After all, this is my story, and it was right about this point in it that I was finding a new beginning.

I started taking baby steps toward a new way of thinking that eventually led to a new kind of happiness. I already knew that no amount of material stuff could bring contentment. I'd seen sad people frantically acquiring more and more jewels, houses, clothes, cars, vacation properties, booze, drugs, food . . . and still feeling empty inside. And I was realizing, too, that no human relationship—even if it seems "perfect"—can really satisfy the deepest longings of a person's soul.

This was radical for me.

After all, I'd been on a lifelong quest to feel good about myself based on who I was with. When I was a young girl, I'd try to get close to a certain uncle whenever he was visiting. He was a war hero who'd received a Congressional Medal of Honor, and when I was sitting next to him at the dinner table, I felt special because he was special. I remembered how I longed for attention from my parents. No matter how much they gave, I always wanted more hugs, more applause, more assurances that I was their most amazing child. When I got a little older, I always had a boyfriend by my side until Alan came into the picture . . . and ever since then, how I felt about myself had depended on how I thought Alan felt about me.

No more. Little, tiny, tender shoots of new growth were peeking out of my soul. The devastation of Alan's departure was leading to a new beginning, new freedom, and the utter security of a new love I had looked for all my life.

Chapter 14

LETTING GO

❧

O soul, are you weary and troubled?
No light in the darkness you see?
There's light for a look at the Savior,
And life more abundant and free!

Turn your eyes upon Jesus,
Look full in His wonderful face;
And the things of earth will grow strangely dim
In the light of His glory and grace.

Helen H. Lemmel,
"Turn Your Eyes Upon Jesus"

Sometimes on golden fall afternoons I walk down to the huge oak tree that has guarded the river at the edge of our property for more than five hundred years. It was there before Tennessee became a state, long before the United States of America even existed.

Around the time Christopher Columbus sailed his wooden ships toward the New World, an acorn the size of a thimble sent a tiny green shoot into the soil we now call ours. Rains came and watered the small sprout. Shawnee Indians floated down the river in long canoes. Hunters killed deer near the riverbank and scraped their hides with hard, white flints we sometimes find buried in the soil today.

The sapling grew, sending its roots deeper and deeper into the earth. Its branches became home to birds and squirrels. Its trunk widened over the decades. Centuries passed, and its upper branches reached toward heaven. Wild storms tossed it; the blazing sun scorched it; the raging river flooded it. But still the tree stood firm.

> Maybe it took Alan's leaving to really rivet my attention on the One who would never leave me. I had only the tiniest mustard seed of faith . . . but in the end, God used it to build a stable home for all of us.

Sometimes when I look up at that massive oak, I can't help but think of how Jesus talked about trees. He slept under the stars and lived most of His life outside, so it makes sense that He'd tie spiritual truths to nature's everyday sights.

"The kingdom of heaven is like a mustard seed," Jesus said. "Though it is the smallest of all your seeds, yet when it grows, it is the largest of garden plants and becomes a tree, so that the birds of the air come and perch in its branches."[1]

Today, when I stare up at the blue skies above the great tree, I think back to the point in my life when my husband left and the storm winds blew. I wasn't much of a tree; I was more like a twig. I had just begun to put my roots back down in the faith of my youth. I was just beginning to turn my eyes to Jesus, to consider what was really important in life. I had been distracted for many years by the passing pleasures and pressures of this world, but now I was coming home, so to speak.

Maybe it took Alan's leaving to really rivet my attention on the One who would never leave me. I had only the tiniest mustard seed of faith . . . but in the end, God used it to build a stable home for all of us.

Putting My Roots Down Deep

During the early days of our separation, I continued life's normal routines. Mattie and Ali went to school; baby Dani was a wonderful comfort. But my strongest means of support and growth came from my relationships with the women in my weekly Bible study.

Jane, the friend from the girls' school who hosted the study, was our organizer. Raised in Memphis, she was (and is) the epitome of Southern graciousness. We jokingly called her "Mother Jane"; she was the mother duck who kept the rest of us in line when we waddled off-topic. We'd meet in Jane's cozy family room, sitting in a circle, some of us dressed for the day, and some in sweats and no makeup. The casualness and security came from the long-standing bond that we had with each other. We went through a study called *Breaking Free,* authored by the wonderful Bible teacher Beth Moore.

Each week our group would dig into sections of the Bible that focused on freedom. We'd talk about our struggles and the things that held us to earth and bound us tight. Then we'd sit in that circle, hold hands, and pray.

I hadn't grown up praying out loud in a setting like this. It felt weird and uncomfortable at first. So did the practice of talking with others about my thoughts and feelings. But I'd always been an eager student, and the academic part of me loved studying the Bible and answering questions in the study guide. I had been spiritually dry for so long that I was dying for truth. I was so thirsty and hungry for God, and I could taste His presence in this little circle of women who loved Him too. So I became more and more free to be the real me—even as I was discovering who the real me really was!

I often broke down in tears during our sharing time. I didn't dish dirt on Alan or tell the others all the particulars of what I was going through, but in that circle of friends, I felt safe to show my hurting heart and know that all of them would treat it tenderly. They cared for me and encouraged me, and I tried to do the same for them.

But this wasn't just a support group, wonderful as such groups can be. Most importantly, the women there shared a common commitment to God. They knew *He* was the only One who could truly help any of us, because only God had the supernatural power to change us. We weren't just focused on each other; we were all focused on Him, and as we learned more about Him and drew closer to Him, we drew closer to one another as well.

Lifeline

I'd had lots of friends and acquaintances, but I hadn't had really close girlfriends for many years. I grew to know and love these friends on a deeper level. They weren't part of the country music world; their husbands were real estate developers, physical therapists, and businessmen. It was casual; no one made anything over me or the situation I was in. But these sisters were rock-solid there for me. They loved me, cried and laughed with me, and pleaded with God to restore my marriage and shower His love on me.

Liz was the youngest in our group, full of life, always with a dramatic tale to tell about her cat, her dogs, or a family member. Her brown eyes sparkled when she shared her stories with us. But Liz had been through deep waters; her husband, a young NASCAR driver, had been killed in a helicopter accident a few years earlier.

In the aftermath of that tragedy, Liz had moved to Nashville with her two young children. As she healed from her horrible loss, and found new strength in her relationship with God, we all prayed that Liz would meet a godly man who would love her children. A few years later, God answered those prayers in the form of a wonderful man who loved God, cherished Liz, and was crazy about Liz's children. They married and went on to have a child.

Beth was a very petite friend with a big heart and an infectious laugh. We joked about her small size: "How can her organs all fit in that teeny-tiny frame?" She was always doing things for other people, and was and is an extremely loyal friend. Our group has prayed with her through many family illnesses and supported her as she faithfully stood by her best friend, whose lengthy battle with cancer finally took her life.

Joy had such a love for the Lord and a deep knowledge of the Bible. She had a dry, self-deprecating sense of humor that always made us laugh. As we danced on the edge of middle age, she was the first of us to break out the reading glasses, and we all relished giving her a hard time about it. We also prayed in tears with her when her husband died in a private plane accident and stood by her at the funerals of each of her parents. We have watched her faith grow through these difficult times.

Kim was the one we could always count on. She continues to be one of my closest friends today. She would pick up any of our kids if we were running late to get them at school. She was the first person we could call if an emergency came up. Our group encouraged her as her husband went through various career challenges in a demanding business. Her faith has been a shining example for all of us.

The second Beth in our group was bubbly, with a blonde, bobbed haircut. She always had a smile on her face and would tell hilarious stories about living in an all-male house with three rambunctious boys and her husband. It was an unwritten rule that on her birthday and Christmas, we showered her with everything pink. With her husband traveling most of the time with his job, she was a wonderful example of strength as she managed her lively household.

As I spent time with these women, in church and in the Sunday school class, I was also studying the Bible. Much of it was familiar, as it is to those of us who grew up in a Southern Baptist church. As a young girl in Sunday school, I'd memorized all the right verses and excelled at "sword drills"—contests to see who could find particular verses of Scripture in the least amount of time.

But now the Scripture wasn't just a matter of knowing the right rote answers. It was coming alive for me in a brand-new way. I was beginning to see it as a love story about how God had loved people from the very beginnings of time. He had so loved all of us that He actually made a way for our sins to be washed clean and our souls to be set free, through Jesus. That wasn't just a one-time understanding at age twelve or whenever one walked the aisle to publicly acknowledge one's faith. It was a day-to-day, living reality.

I was also beginning to see that this Gospel was all about grace—the undeserved favor we receive from God—not about our performance. It didn't matter how good I'd been or how lovely I looked: God loved me with a wild, intimate, overwhelming love just because He did . . . not because of anything I did. Even as my heart was like a big bruise inside of me because of Alan's leaving, I was beginning to hear the chords of a new song, a song I'd never heard before, a sweet whisper that was telling me all would be well.

> EVEN AS MY HEART WAS LIKE A BIG BRUISE INSIDE OF ME BECAUSE OF ALAN'S LEAVING, I WAS BEGINNING TO HEAR THE CHORDS OF A NEW SONG, A SONG I'D NEVER HEARD BEFORE, A SWEET WHISPER THAT WAS TELLING ME ALL WOULD BE WELL.

Still, though, at that point it was just a whisper.

A Bigger Prayer

One day after Sunday school was over, I sought out the teacher. Robert Wolgemuth was in the publishing industry, a compassionate man with a deep knowledge of the Scriptures and a mellow, soothing voice. His beautiful wife, Bobbie, bubbled with the love of God. We found a quiet corner in the back of the big room, and I told them exactly what my problem was . . . or so I thought.

"I'm Alan Jackson's wife," I began. "We're separated. Could you pray with me that he would come back?"

The Wolgemuths weren't part of the country music world, and had to ask someone later who Alan Jackson was, but they put their arms around me. Bobbie's expressive face was full of compassion, and Robert prayed for God's love to flow over me.

Over the next few weeks, Bobbie would seek me out at Sunday school.

"How are you doing?" she would ask, and I knew she really cared.

"Please keep praying," I'd say. "Pray that Alan will come back!"

By this point Bobbie felt comfortable enough with me to be very straightforward.

"Denise," she said, "we love you and we are so *for* you. But we need to pray a different prayer. A *bigger* prayer. We need to pray not that Alan will come back, but that you will be the woman God is calling you to be. Of course we want Alan to come back. But that's secondary. The first thing right now is that you seek God with all your heart. My prayer will be that God will show you what incredible love He has for you."

I knew that Bobbie was right, and just about half of me was willing to pray that prayer. The other half of me just wanted Alan back. Period.

But I found out a great thing about God. He doesn't require that we become *completely* willing. He doesn't wait until our faith or our motives are absolutely pure and perfect. If He did, He'd wait forever, and while He has the time to do so, we don't. He took my small surrenders, my little steps of willingness, and began to do little miracles with them.

It's like the story of the boy in the New Testament who suffered from epilepsy.[2] His father brought him to Jesus. By this point the boy was probably a young man; the father had gone through many long years of heartbreak and frustration.

Convulsing, the boy foamed at the mouth and rolled on the ground, his arms flailing.

"How long has he been like this?" Jesus asked the father.

"From childhood," said the father. "But if you can do anything, take pity on us and help us."

" '*If you can*'?" Jesus repeated. "Everything is possible for him who believes."

I can't imagine the horrible pressure the father felt at that point. Was Jesus saying that his son's healing depended on how much faith he had? There was no way he could rack up enough "belief" to score a healing. His heart constricted, and his years of pain and fear overflowed.

"I do believe!" he shouted to Jesus. "Help me overcome my unbelief!"

And Jesus healed his son.

I love that story because of the father's raw honesty, and

Jesus' response to it. So I prayed my own version of the father's words.

"O Lord," I'd say, "I am willing for You to change me. And please help me overcome my *un*willingness!"

After a lifetime of trying to be "perfect" in so many ways, suffering from the "disease to please," it was healing to realize that I didn't have to have perfect faith! I could admit my insufficiency and ask God for what I needed. And I was beginning to believe that He would give it to me.

So I prayed, stiffly at first, and then more and more passionately, that God would give me the desire to change. I prayed that He would shape me into the unique person He had created me to be. I desperately wanted Alan back, of course. And part of me was constantly trying to figure out how to fix our marriage, fix

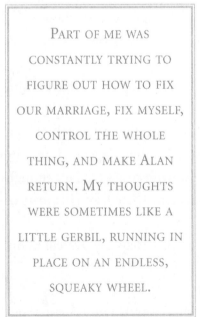

PART OF ME WAS CONSTANTLY TRYING TO FIGURE OUT HOW TO FIX OUR MARRIAGE, FIX MYSELF, CONTROL THE WHOLE THING, AND MAKE ALAN RETURN. MY THOUGHTS WERE SOMETIMES LIKE A LITTLE GERBIL, RUNNING IN PLACE ON AN ENDLESS, SQUEAKY WHEEL.

myself, control the whole thing, and make Alan return. My thoughts were sometimes like a little gerbil, running in place on an endless, squeaky wheel.

Meanwhile, my friends were praying. Bobbie and Robert were praying. And I, with a faltering heart but a little shred of faith, was praying that God would give me the will to want His will. No matter what.

So maybe I shouldn't have

been surprised when those prayers were answered, right in the middle of a routine morning.

Surrender!

I was driving the girls to school, not really listening while they were jabbering with each other in the backseat. My mind was a whirl, as usual. I dropped them off, blew kisses and waved good-bye, and talked out loud to God.

"Okay, Lord," I cried. "I am so tired! I can't manage this situation. I can't control what happens or doesn't happen in my marriage. I can't make Alan come back. I can't believe it's Your will that our family break up. But I can't take this anymore!"

In that moment, I totally turned my eyes toward Jesus.

"I give up!" I sobbed. "I give in! I know You'll take care of me; I am letting go of it all, and You'll just have to get me through."

I sobbed and drove home to my empty mansion. It was the first time in my life that I had *completely* let go of *my* will. I relinquished my desires. My need to try to cling to Alan at all costs. I totally let go and gave it all to God. It was the first time I had actually trusted Him to totally run my life, no matter what the outcome.

No angels danced on my dashboard. No rays of light shone through my giant diamond to make a rainbow of hope on my windshield. But for the first time, I had a tiny, sure sense of real peace. *Peace* . . . in spite of my circumstances. It was like there was a connection between heaven and earth in that otherwise ordinary moment.

It's odd: I would never have chosen to go through the pain of those awful days, but through it, God got my attention. I had been skimming along on the surface of my fairy-tale life, ignoring the fact that Jesus was softly and tenderly calling me to come home to Him. I'd closed my eyes to any warnings that a storm was coming in my marriage.

Once that storm broke my heart wide open, though, I finally cried out to God. I heard His voice. I felt His love. And I realized that Alan was never designed to be the center of my life. No human being could fill that place. Christ alone could truly be my all-in-all.

Chapter 15

PRAYING NEW PRAYERS

⌒◈⌒

This is what the LORD says—he who made a way through the sea,
a path through the mighty waters . . .
"Forget the former things; do not dwell on the past.
See, I am doing a new thing!
Now it springs up; do you not perceive it?
I am making a way in the desert and streams in the wasteland."

Isaiah 43:16, 18–19

The old oak tree on our property changes with the seasons. In the fall it is warm and mellow, standing tall in a thicket of golden trees. In the winter its leaves all fall. It looks dead and stark against the cold, gray skies. In the spring it sends forth tender growth, and green leaves return to cover its naked branches. In the sweltering summer it offers cool shade beneath its big canopy.

When I look at that big tree, or consider the flocks of cherry trees that dot our pastures in the spring, like lacy lambs, I think of seasons in my own life.

The separation from Alan was like winter for me. It felt cold and dry as a dead bone. But under the surface, down in the very marrow of who I was, God was actually growing something tender and new in me. His Spirit was flowing, and springtime was coming.

I felt like the description in Psalm 1:1–3:

> Blessed is the [person] who does not walk in the
> counsel of the wicked . . .
> But his delight is in the law of the LORD,
> And on his law he meditates day and night.
> He is like a tree planted by streams of water,
> Which yields its fruit in season
> And whose leaf does not wither.
> Whatever he does prospers.

In a worldly sense, plenty of people would give me "wicked counsel" about Alan.

"Just get what you can," they'd say. "Get the best lawyer money can buy, and take Alan for everything you can get." Others would tell me, "Let Alan know that you don't care. Make sure he sees you with someone else."

They meant well, but besides sounding like we were back in high school or something, these bits of advice were actually unhealthy ways of looking at the situation. They were all about retribution and gain, fueled by rage.

Not that I hadn't considered them all at some point!

But I had seen women who'd been wronged get to the point where any conversation with them seethed with bitterness and rage. They were always negative, unable to move past their anger to a new start.

No Baseball Bat

Anger came quite naturally to me. At one point I threw all of Alan's remaining clothes into the back of a pickup truck so a friend could dump them at his rental home. If he was not going to live with me, then I could at least have more closet space.

More often I beat him up with words. (Thankfully, I never did take a Louisville Slugger to any of his vehicles' headlights, as Carrie Underwood sings in her hit song about revenge, nor did I dump his music awards in the lake.)

But as time went by, a miracle happened. I found myself drawn by God's Spirit into a different response altogether. It wasn't me, as if I became a great heroine far above normal human reactions, Saint Denise of Nashville.

No, I just found that the more I pursued my new relationship with Jesus and the more I explored the Bible, the more my attitudes were changing. It was incredible: I saw the words of Psalm 1 beginning to come true in *me*, of all people. I was finding my "delight" in God's Word.

Instead of my thoughts running like a gerbil on a wheel when I went to bed at night, I'd pray out loud. I'd proclaim God's promises for peace and His love to my empty bedroom. After all, it wasn't like I was keeping Alan awake; he wasn't there. But I wasn't alone. God was with me. And the Bible wasn't a big old dusty book . . . it was God's love letter to me. I could go to sleep in peace as I grabbed hold of His truths in my mind and meditated on them in my heart.

As I did this, I became more like that "tree planted by streams of water" that Psalm 1:3 describes. Drawing my nourishment from the Bible, sustained by God's fresh love, I was growing stronger in the perspective of what really mattered. Faith. Hope. Love.

After all, we become like whatever we pursue. When I'd chased after what other people thought of me, I'd ended up hollow and flimsy, my identity as fleeting as a fashion trend. As I chased after God, I actually found my true self.

> AS I CHASED AFTER GOD, I ACTUALLY FOUND MY TRUE SELF.

I was also reading tons of Christian books. I read *A Love Worth Giving*, by Max Lucado, and underlined the sentence that read, "There are seasons when God allows us to feel the frailty of human love so we'll appreciate the strength of his love."[1] Though I never would have chosen the sad season of separation from my husband, I found that it drove me to the Love that would never let me go. And the more I got into God's powerful love, the more it changed me.

Snipping and Clipping

I was also going through some changes that were, shall we say, a little more superficial.

Soon after Alan left, I sang a few verses of the old song "I Will Survive" and took myself off to the salon. I'd had long, blonde hair ever since Alan first laid eyes on me. "Cut it off!" I told the stylist. I shut my eyes while she clipped and snipped, and kept them closed while she dusted me off and someone came along with a broom and swept all my long, golden locks away to the trash. Then I had them add platinum color to it, just to put it over the top.

> MY HAIR WAS ALMOST WHITE, IT WAS SO LIGHT, AND APPROXIMATELY HALF AN INCH LONG. I LOOKED LIKE JOAN OF ARC, OR MAYBE A PLATINUM VERSION OF DEMI MOORE IN *G.I. JANE.*

Eventually, since I needed to drive home, I opened my eyes. My hair was almost white, it was so light, and approximately half an inch long. I looked like Joan of Arc, or maybe a platinum version of Demi Moore in *G.I. Jane.* I looked like I had joined the Army.

I marched home. Fortunately the girls loved me whether I had hair or not . . . especially Dani, who was about six months old. I guess her vision wasn't fully developed yet.

Only God Knows

During this surreal time that Daddy was gone and Mommy was crying, laughing, going to Bible study, and cutting off her hair, all of us drew great comfort from baby Dani. It was so soothing to simply tickle her and make her smile, to hug her and kiss her and know that she loved me unconditionally.

Like me, Dani had been a twin. Months before, at my eleven-week checkup, I had my first ultrasound. Alan was with me, and he noticed that there were two "peanut shapes" inside me. He asked the nurse if there were two babies, but she didn't really answer.

"I'll get the doctor to take a look," she said. When the doctor looked at the screen, he confirmed that there were indeed two babies . . . but one was not viable. "This is what we call a 'disappearing twin,'" he said gently. "It happens every once in a while."

For whatever reason, the little fetus had stopped growing. While Dani's heart was beating strong, her twin's heart had gone still. His tissue would eventually break down and be absorbed into the uterine lining.

The joy of celebrating the one baby, and the grief of losing the other, seemed like it foreshadowed the extreme roller-coaster of emotions that my heart would experience in the coming months. I often thought sadly of the twin who disappeared. Would Dani have had a twin brother like I had? I didn't know why he didn't grow. Sometimes I wondered if having twins during this period of terrible stress would have been too much for me to handle. Only God knows.

But the mystery of it all reminded me that God is far greater than I can imagine. I can't understand His ways. In sorrow and loss, as well as in joy, I always have a choice to make. I can choose to believe that He is good, and in control, and to trust Him . . . or I can try to manipulate every outcome and rigidly try to control my own life. During this sad time of separation from Alan, it was becoming clearer and clearer to me that I couldn't *say* that I trusted God to be in charge of my life and then grab back the steering wheel whenever I didn't understand what He was doing.

Special Because . . .

One day at Bible study, Jane told us we were doing a craft for the day. We did not argue with Mother Jane. She got out sheets of clean white paper, and we all took a sheet for each of our children. I started with Mattie. At the top I wrote, "Mattie is special because . . ." and then I listed ten wonderful things about our oldest daughter.

But the first thing on the list was not about Mattie, per se, but about God. "Mattie is special because she is a child of God."

Then I made a list for Ali, starting with "Ali is special because she is a child of God." Then I made one for baby Dani, though she could not yet read.

Then God nudged my heart. I asked for another sheet of paper. This one was for my husband. At the top I wrote, "Alan is special because he is a child of God." Then I listed other reasons why Alan was loved, including the fact that "he is a great father," because he was. And is.

At any rate, I made these four plaques, put them in eight by

> ALL I KNEW WAS THAT FOR SOME REASON I HAD A NEW STRENGTH AND FREEDOM INSIDE, AND I WASN'T AS INTERESTED IN CLINGING TO ALAN TO FIND OUT IF HE WAS GOING TO COME BACK TO ME.

ten frames, and hid them for my family to find. Later that day, Alan happened to stop by to pick up something from the house.

"Daddy!" Mattie yelled after she'd hugged him hello, "Mommy made us each something! She hid them in our closets! She made you one, too!"

Alan went upstairs and looked in his closet. He came down holding the plaque to his chest. I didn't know what he was thinking. All I knew was that for some reason I had a new strength and freedom inside, and I wasn't as interested in clinging to Alan to find out if he was going to come back to me.

But I *was* interested in letting him know that God loved him, no matter what. I knew that as a songwriter, Alan loved words, and so I wanted to communicate with him in a way he could appreciate. The simple words on his little plaque showed him that something was changing inside of me. It was because I was rooting my life in the "law of the Lord," as Psalm 1:2 puts it. I was drawing my identity from God, not from Alan, and not from the world around me. It was wild, and I'd never felt so free.

Later Bobbie told me, in her truthful yet supportive way, "Denise, when I first met you, you were such a weak, needy person. Now you're becoming this strong, creative woman who devours the Bible. You're radiant. You're amazing!"

During this period, Alan often came and went. He'd stop by

the house to get more clothes, or something he'd forgotten, or to trade whatever he was driving for a different car. One day he came to get something, and I was in the kitchen, sitting on the floor with Dani and playing with her.

Usually if I knew Alan was going to come by, I'd do my hair—what was left of it—and try to put on something cute. Old habits die hard, and I wanted to look good for him.

But on this day I had on an old warm-up suit. No makeup. I was playing with Dani, tickling her and making her laugh, fully in the moment, and I was only vaguely aware of Alan, his long frame standing in the doorway. He just leaned there, watching us. And then the next time I looked up, he was gone.

The next day, Alan called me.

"Denise," he said, "yesterday when I was watching you on the kitchen floor with the baby, there was something different about you. It was like you had this warm glow all around you."

I was floored, but I knew my "glow" wasn't from me. It was from God's presence in my heart. As I was living in a day-by-day way that was plugged into His power, He was the one lighting up the kitchen.

When Alan finally spoke again, I heard an echo of the boy I'd met in high school.

"Nisey, could we go out for a date this weekend?"

"Okay," I said.

Chapter 16

TAKING SMALL STEPS

❧

What a fellowship, what a joy divine,
Leaning on the everlasting arms;
What a blessedness, what a peace is mine,
Leaning on the everlasting arms.

What have I to dread, what have I to fear,
Leaning on the everlasting arms?
I have blessed peace with my Lord so near,
Leaning on the everlasting arms.

Elisha A. Hoffman,
"Leaning on the Everlasting Arms"

Trust in the LORD with all your heart
and lean not on your own understanding;
in all your ways acknowledge him,
and he will make your paths straight.

Proverbs 3:5–6

*A*s I dressed to go out to dinner with Alan, my thoughts whirled around like a snowstorm on a windy day. Staring in the big mirrors in our master bath, I applied eye shadow. *How could Alan dare to ask me out when he was so sure that we weren't right for each other?* I asked the mirror. *Hasn't he said, on and off throughout the years, that something just wasn't right? How can he suddenly be questioning his decision that our marriage was over? Is he just pouring salt into my raw emotional wounds?*

I didn't know if my heart could survive the evening.

But as I put on mascara, I thought that at least I knew by now what my heart was feeling. I knew I wanted to be with Alan more than anything. Up until now, we had talked very little about the prospect of staying together. But all the weeks of being alone had really made me realize how much I did love him, how I longed for his touch, how I still wanted him as my lover, my friend, and my companion for the rest of my life. I had nothing to lose, really, if I went to dinner with him, and everything to lose if I didn't go because I was afraid I'd be hurt.

Thoroughly conflicted, I applied my lipstick, grabbed a jacket, and went downstairs.

There was a little tap on our kitchen door, and Alan walked in as the girls were having their dinner. Their eyes lit up when they realized that Daddy and Mommy were actually going out together. It all felt incredibly odd to me . . . as if I was somehow reliving our first date in high school, yet here we were, with three little girls and an eighteen-year marriage under our belt. Part of me felt as though Mother and Daddy would be waiting up for me if I got home past my curfew. We kissed our girls good night and drove to the restaurant.

Our Second "First Date"

The emotional blizzard continued. We settled into our table at Merchants, which was private enough that we shouldn't be disturbed, but also lively enough that we shouldn't have to worry about anyone eavesdropping on our conversation. At first we were quite civil and kept things on the surface. I told Alan little stories about Dani beginning to crawl, and how Mattie and Ali could make her laugh by the silly things they'd do. We talked about how the older girls were doing in school.

Then Alan finally asked, "How do they seem to be doing with the separation?"

So much for civilized conversation.

"What do you mean?" I sputtered. "Their whole world has been torn apart, and you ask how they're doing? Why don't you ask them how it feels to suddenly have your daddy move out, and see what they say? Why don't you tell them all the things that are wrong with me so maybe they'll understand that your leaving us was not my idea? Why don't you tell them why I've been crying for the last three months?"

When I finally stopped to take a breath, I heard an entirely different response than I had expected. Instead of lashing back at me, Alan looked at me steadily.

"Denise," he said humbly, "I'm really sorry for all the pain

> I LOOKED INTO HIS
>
> BLUE EYES AND KNEW
>
> THAT I STILL WANTED
>
> HIM MORE THAN
>
> I COULD SAY.
>
> BUT HOW COULD I
>
> ERASE ALL THE PAIN
>
> HE HAD CAUSED ME
>
> AND THE CHILDREN BY
>
> THE SEPARATION?

I've caused you and the girls by moving out. But I just couldn't continue pretending everything was okay when it wasn't. I'm still real confused, but I do think I'm willing to go to counseling with you to try to figure everything out."

My flip-flopping heart flipped back toward Alan. I looked into his blue eyes and knew that I still wanted him more than I could say. But how could I erase all the pain he had caused me and the children by the separation? Yet I was thrilled to hear him offer a glimmer of hope to my wounded spirit.

In between these heights and depths, we managed to pick at our food, but decided to skip dessert. Neither of us had much of an appetite.

As tense and awkward as I felt that evening, I knew in my heart that I still loved Alan, no matter what, and that I would do anything to restore our marriage. He drove me home. Then, on the porch next to our kitchen, he kissed me good night, not a polite peck, but passionately enough for me to know that he missed me too.

Crossroads

That strange date was a crossroads. When I began to realize that Alan might actually be willing to try to reconcile, I began to think about all the positive growth that had come from our time apart.

For the first time in my married life, I felt some sort of identity apart from Alan. I was making decisions on my own that I had never made before. Some of these sound ridiculously insignificant now . . . but back then my self-confidence was so low that any decision apart from Alan was almost impossible. So, during our separation, when I actually went to the Ford dealership where Alan had always bought our trucks, and bought a new Expedition, it was a big step for me.

And as I drove that big blue SUV home, I remembered that blue used to be my favorite color. This sounds absurd, but at that time it was an emotional revelation. I had actually picked something based on what *I* liked and wanted, not on what I thought Alan would like. Gradually, I was beginning to rediscover pieces of myself that I had long forgotten—even if it was something as simple as recalling my favorite color.

This small, new pleasure in self-discovery showed some of the ruts we'd gotten into. Alan wanted me to make my own decisions, to be bold about my preferences. But his personality was such that *his* preferences were quite strong and entrenched. He had opinions about everything, and if someone didn't share his view, he knew just how to argue him into it. I'd drive myself crazy trying to please him, trying to make my decisions based on what I thought *he* would prefer—since his preferences were "best." It was so freeing not to be consumed with trying to guess what Alan would want.

If he did come back home, would I have the confidence not to fall back into that passive way of relating to him? Further, were there parts of his personality that I actually resented for the way I allowed them to control me? I knew I loved Alan. But did I really *like* him?

Seeking Counsel

I had started seeing a Christian counselor as soon as Alan moved out of the house. I looked forward to every session, hoping that some magical remedy would reveal itself. As the sessions continued week after week, I became more and more frustrated. I did not want to talk about my family history, how I had felt as a child, or anything else that I thought didn't pertain directly—and quickly—to my relationship with Alan. Here I was, my marriage on the verge of dissolving: I didn't have the energy or patience to go back to square one in my youth and work through all my inner issues. I wanted a quick fix.

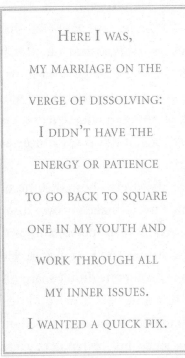

HERE I WAS, MY MARRIAGE ON THE VERGE OF DISSOLVING: I DIDN'T HAVE THE ENERGY OR PATIENCE TO GO BACK TO SQUARE ONE IN MY YOUTH AND WORK THROUGH ALL MY INNER ISSUES. I WANTED A QUICK FIX.

When Alan went with me to see the counselor, as he had promised, I was very defensive. We'd sit in big wingback chairs, both facing the therapist, not looking at each other. I wanted to relate in great detail exactly how Alan had hurt me, and give complete histories and analyses of all his flaws. When Alan's turn came, he was quite skilled at listing all the many reasons that our marriage was so much less than he wanted it to be.

Both of us finally had a captive audience—the poor counselor—and each of us wanted to win the debate. Meanwhile, after meeting with us, the therapist himself probably wanted to go off and get some counseling, or at least down a few stiff drinks.

It did not take very long to realize that this method of dealing with the problem was not going to get us anywhere.

Taken Apart to Be Put Back Together

As I saw Alan's patience wearing thin, I began to worry that he was going to bail out on me and the counseling altogether. I felt like a time bomb was ticking, and the longer we were separated, the less likely it was that we'd get back together. I told the therapist that things were moving too slowly. Was there anyone he knew who would be willing to do some intensive work with us—someone who could peel our marriage onion down to its innermost layer, so to speak, in the quickest amount of time? The counselor, no doubt thrilled to get rid of us and send us far, far away, suggested a St. Louis couple who were both psychotherapists.

We made an appointment and drove to St. Louis. It felt awkward to go to this couple's house (which we had chosen, given the option of their home or their offices), but it felt safe and private too. They were about our ages, dressed casually, like college psychology professors. Their modest home was in a natural, woodsy setting. We spent the weekend with them, leaving only to go to a nearby hotel to sleep.

At first, I talked with the wife, and Alan talked with the husband. Separately. This way they could hear each account without the interference of the other spouse. (The Nashville counselor must have clued them in that this approach would be necessary.)

Then we all met together. They seemed to be assessing all the data they'd collected and analyzing how we interacted. Was there hope, or should we just move to separate planets?

In the end, they gave their conclusion. There was hope. In their expert opinion, we were indeed compatible. We shared the same beliefs, goals, and desires for our family and our marriage. Success would now depend on how willing we were to humbly unlearn some old ways of communicating that had damaged our relationship and replace them with new ways of interacting with each other.

All this was totally exhausting, like doing a year's worth of therapy in one weekend. It even included a hypnosis session. I was pretty skeptical about this, but again, I was willing to do whatever might help us get to the core of the issues we faced.

I lay down on a sofa while the therapist talked with me quietly. There was no swinging pocket watch, and I did not stagger around the room like a sleepwalker. I did, however, enter into a relaxed state in which I felt very free to talk about whatever was asked me. I remember crying. I talked about how much I loved Alan, and how amazing I had always thought he was. I talked about my lifelong need to feel like I was good enough, and how I'd never really felt that I measured up. I said I'd always wanted to please my father, and then Alan, above everyone else. I said there was a depth of love I'd longed for but never completely felt.

After this session—in which I thankfully did not drool heavily or reveal anything that was *too* embarrassing—I was so emotionally drained that I literally could not stand up on my own. My legs were too exhausted.

But even though my limbs were weak, Alan saw an inner strength in me that he hadn't glimpsed since our dating days. He saw my determination to make our marriage work, as well

> ALAN SAW AN INNER STRENGTH IN ME THAT HE HADN'T GLIMPSED SINCE OUR DATING DAYS. HE SAW MY DETERMINATION TO MAKE OUR MARRIAGE WORK, AS WELL AS AN INTENSITY THAT MADE HIM REALIZE THAT I WOULD SURVIVE, NO MATTER WHAT.

as an intensity that made him realize that I would survive, no matter what. That strength was one of the things that had attracted him to me when we first met so many years earlier. And he also saw my willingness to forgive and put the past behind us.

As we left St. Louis, I felt a sense of relief and accomplishment that maybe we finally understood the big picture and knew what we needed to do to rebuild a healthy marriage. I was beginning to understand some things about Alan that I just hadn't realized before.

For example, no matter how many awards he got or how many fans were cheering him on, he needed to hear affirmation from me. He needed to hear my love and respect, both just between us and also in front of our friends. "What everyone else says about how good I am doesn't really matter," he said. "*You're the one I need to hear it from!*"

He'd told me that many times over the years, but it hadn't sunk in. Now I was beginning to get the fact that my superstar husband needed affirmation from, yes, little old me!

I'd been raised with parents who loved each other, but didn't hug or kiss much in front of their kids. I'd never heard them build each other up with sweet words. They may well have done that in private, of course, but when I was growing up, I just didn't have a model of a husband and wife regularly expressing love and affection. As a result I had a habitual reserve about me, an inner distance that had affected Alan more than I'd ever realized.

Questions and Fears

It was great to have a sense of optimism about new revelations in our marriage. But the closer we got to Nashville, the more afraid I felt. If Alan moved back home, could our union survive and really be different after almost eighteen years? I could not think of even one couple I knew whose marriage had been restored after separation. But I knew of plenty of people who had given up on their marriage after crisis, infidelity, or simple estrangement and discontentment. Even people who had tried to work at it had eventually ended up going their separate ways.

Could we really be different? Or would we end up in the same situation as so many of our friends and acquaintances? I already knew the awkwardness of showing up at Mattie's basketball games only to worry about where I could sit to be away from Alan. It was stilted, embarrassing, and sad. But that kind of perpetual discomfort was everyday reality for many families we knew.

I'd also seen the resentment and hostility that sometimes settles in for couples after the divorce is final. I'd watched children become the mediators between their parents. I certainly did not want that for our family.

Even as I felt a chill of fear about our future, I thought about my girlfriends in my prayer group. I felt reassured, realizing that this really wasn't solely dependent on us—one false move and we'd be doomed. God was doing something here. My friends had not stopped praying for us since the first day I told them that Alan was leaving. They never stopped encouraging me and reminding me that all things are possible with God.

Every night since our separation, I had prayed Scriptures, claiming God's promises for me and asking Him to restore my marriage. If He wanted our family to stay together, then I had to believe that He had the power to make that happen. Hard as it was for me to acknowledge, I couldn't control the outcome. And incredibly, I was beginning to come to peace with that.

My favorite Santa picture (1998)

Alan's parents, Ruth and Eugene, at a CMA after-show party
Tony Phipps Photography

Our-500-year-old natural wonder on a snowy day

Us posing under our tree
Wendi Webb Thomas Photography

Alan and me in the A.C. Cobra on the New England 1000 Road Rally (May 1999)

My prayer group at Liz's
wedding. From left—
Beth J, Jane, Kim, Liz,
me, Beth I, and Joy
(May 2000)
Helen Burrus Photography

Alan and his sisters with Mama
Ruth at Carol's wedding.
From left—Carol, Connie, Alan,
Diane and Cathy
(June 2000)
Bob Fraley Photography

My 40th birthday at
Little Palm Island
(2000)

R to L: Me, Mother, my siblings, Danny and Jane

Our family on the set of the "Drive" video (2002)
Tony Phipps Photography

36th Annual CMA Awards. Alan won five awards, including
"Entertainer of the Year"
Photo by Jim Hagens, CMA

Alan accepting "Entertainer of the Year" Award at
2003 CMA Awards show
Photo by John Russell, CMA

Us on the set of "Let It Be Christmas" TV Special (2002)
Tony Phipps Photography

Alan and me at home being interviewed for
"Let It Be Christmas" TV Special (2002)
Tony Phipps Photography

Ali and Dani ready to perform on Alan's TV special
"Let It Be Christmas" (2002)
Tony Phipps Photography

My daddy holding an auction item
for Angel's House in Newnan, GA
(an autographed hat of Alan's)

On the red carpet at the
Country Music Awards Show 2006
Photo by Jim Hagans, CMA

MERRY CHRISTMAS
THE JACKSONS

Our 2006 Christmas card

Chapter 17

COMING HOME

✧

Softly and tenderly Jesus is calling,
Calling for you and for me.
See, on the portals, He's waiting and watching;
Watching for you and for me.

Come home, come home,
Ye who are weary come home;
Earnestly, tenderly, Jesus is calling;
Calling, "O sinner, come home!"

Will L. Thompson,
"Softly and Tenderly"

The Bible says that if you have even as much faith as a tiny mustard seed and tell a mountain to move, it will. I had no interest in rearranging any geography, but there were mountains in both Alan and me that needed to change. I knew that God had the power to transform us, if we were willing.

Deep inside, I knew that the One I had given my life to at age twelve was not going to let me down. He was with me, no matter what. He was stronger than the challenges we faced. I could trust in Him. Even though I couldn't see how our story was going to turn out, I knew that the end was in His hands.

During this time, my friend Bobbie was praying faithfully for us. Every morning she got up while it was still dark outside. She'd sit at her kitchen table, her open Bible in front of her, and write her prayers in her journal.

"March 3, 1998," she wrote as she read Psalm 46. "God is our refuge and strength, an ever-present help in trouble. Therefore we will not fear, though the earth give way and the mountains fall into the heart of the sea . . . There is a river whose streams make glad the . . . holy place where the Most High dwells. God is within her, she will not fall; God will help her at break of day.

"Lord," wrote Bobbie, "I pray that Denise may be comforted in the holy place, where the Most High dwells . . . that You will be with Denise, that she will not fall. Today, Lord, please wake Denise up with confidence that the Lord Almighty will be her fortress. As she prepares the day for Mattie, Ali, and Dani, let Denise be still and know that You are God!"

Powerful Prayers

Prayer is such a mystery. We don't know how it "works," how God hears prayers offered up to Him on our behalf and then changes the course of our lives. All I know is that the invisible, whispered prayers of friends, acquaintances, and even Alan's fans were drawing me ever closer to the enormous love and power of God. It was supernatural. It made me realize how connected believers really are. We can have a mysterious unity of spirit, purpose, and communication that exceeds the bonds of friendships that exist solely on a human level.

During these months I read Stormie Omartian's book, *The Power of a Praying Wife.* Each chapter gives Scripture verses and prayers that pertain to specific areas of a husband's life—his protection, salvation, fidelity, finances, temptations, the whole gamut. Every night after the girls were asleep, I read those portions of the Bible out loud and followed the guidelines in Stormie's book to pray for Alan.[1]

> I WAS BEGINNING TO REALIZE THAT HEARTFELT PRAYERS ARE INCREDIBLY POWERFUL—NOT JUST IN HOW THEY CHANGE OTHER PEOPLE OR CIRCUMSTANCES, BUT IN HOW THEY CHANGE *ME.*

In regard to old choices, I would pray, "Lord, please deliver Alan from the past and from any hold it may have on him. Help him to be renewed in his mind Eph. 4:22–23. Enlarge his understanding to know that You make all things new Rev. 21:5. Redeem his past! Bring life out of it! Heal his wounds, and restore his soul! Ps 147:3 and 23:3."

In regard to our marriage, I'd pray, "God, please protect our marriage from anything that would harm or destroy it. Shield it from our own selfishness and neglect and from unhealthy or dangerous situations. Set us free from past hurts, ties from previous relationships, and unrealistic expectations of one another. Unite us in a bond of friendship, commitment, generosity, and understanding. Please, make our love for each other grow stronger every day!"

I was beginning to realize that heartfelt prayers are incredibly powerful—not just in how they change other people or circumstances, but in how they change *me*. There was no secret formula needed, no "thees" or "thous" or stilted language. The Bible guided me about who God really is, and I realized I could talk with Him as if I were sharing with one of my closest friends, pouring out my heart.

Meanwhile, after our counseling adventures in St. Louis, Alan returned to his rental house and life on the road. We continued to "date," strange as that was. Sometimes we'd go on midday picnics in one of Alan's old convertibles down the Natchez Trace near our house. Or we'd go to our lake house, where we'd take a ride in an old wooden boat, make dinner, and watch a movie. Sometimes we'd just sit in rockers on the porch of our secluded log cabin, talking and watching the river flow by. We both wanted to make sure that we were doing the right thing before Alan moved back home. The separation had been hard enough for Mattie and Ali the first time. I certainly didn't want them to go through that experience again. I didn't want to relive it either.

As distressed as he was, Alan had continued to work during our separation, not wanting to cancel concerts that were already confirmed. Being on the road and focusing on his work gave him some relief from the conflicting emotions churning inside of him. Music also gave him an outlet. Several of the songs that he wrote just before our separation reflected his mood, particularly the aptly named "Gone Crazy."

Gone crazy, goin' out of my mind,
I've asked myself the reasons at least a thousand times.
Goin' up and down this hallway, tryin' to leave the pain behind,
Ever since you left me, I've been gone, gone, gone,
I've been gone.

All kinds of people were listening to lyrics like these and drawing all kinds of conclusions as to what was going on in our private lives. As for me, I couldn't listen to country music on the radio, Alan's songs or anyone else's. They hurt too much.

Meanwhile, the tabloids were having a field day. All kinds of things were printed, most of which were not true. Sometimes friends warned me when they saw something in print about our breakup, so I would hear it from them rather than the media. But I never saw or read any of these sensational stories. It was just too painful.

For the first time in my life, I realized how celebrities must feel when the paparazzi prey on them, hoping to get a picture or information they can sell to the rag magazines. Though I never saw people following me, and no one shoved cameras in my face, Alan saw strange cars parked on the street in front of his rental house after dark. He never knew when someone would pop out of the shadows, flashing a camera.

Before, it had never bothered me for photographers to take pictures of us, or for fans to ask for Alan's autograph. It was usually in a public situation, and it was part of the celebrity lifestyle. Alan had always appreciated the opportunity to thank supporters for liking his music and making his success possible. He never forgot who had put him in the spotlight in the first place.

But now people's tactics and intentions were quite different. These weren't fans. These were "professionals" out to make a buck, invading our private lives with the intention of exploiting our personal heartache. They cared nothing for the real story. Nor could they have appreciated the actual realities that Alan and I were going through.

Ejecting Old Tapes

The counseling was over. We had laid out our relationship on the table, and the counselors had analyzed it all, like doctors probing a big pile of intestines or something. Now it was time to put some of that analysis into action. We were moving from the theoretical to the practical. We knew what was wrong with our old patterns; all we had to do was to create new, healthy habits of interacting with each other.

Easier said than done.

As you know, one of the biggest areas for me had to do with my own self-confidence and comfort in my own skin. I had lots of old tapes playing in my head, with destructive themes like "I'm not good enough" . . . "I'm not Alan's soul mate" . . . "I'll never be the right one for him" . . . "He'll never be happy with me" . . . "I'm so dependent, I could never make it without Alan."

These bad tapes had to be ejected, thrown away, and

replaced with new themes that I downloaded from my relationship with God. Through the words of Scripture, He told me, "Denise, I've loved you with an everlasting love, and I will build you up" . . . "I have great plans for you, and I am doing a new thing to give you new freedoms in your marriage" . . . "My grace is sufficient for you—you have everything you need to make it, for I am strong even when you are weak, and I am with you always!"[2]

I understood how my dependency on Alan had played such a big role in our breakup, and I had seen my confidence increase over the months of our separation. I'd begun to reestablish my own identity apart from him.

For one, friends and acquaintances had been careful not to bring up Alan when I was around. Their conversations had centered more on me and the girls. Thus I found myself responding as an individual, rather than as the junior partner of a power couple.

Similarly, questions from employees and workers regarding our house and extensive grounds were now directed to me since Alan was not around. I found myself in the role of property manager—a role that had always been Alan's. As I continued in that function, I realized that I was becoming a better decision maker, and that I was much more confident in the choices I made.

But again, could I really change the way I had always related to Alan? I was certainly enlightened as to healthy and unhealthy ways of interacting with a spouse, but would I really be able to put this nice, new knowledge into everyday action?

I would only find out the answer after Alan came home.

Home Again

He lived in our log cabin down by the river for a week or two, and then moved back into our home the first week of May. Tears welled up in my eyes as he told the children that he was here to stay.

"Girls, I want you to know something," he said. "Fifty years from now, when you are grown and have families of your own, your mama and I will still be together. You don't need to worry. We'll be right here, sitting in rocking chairs on the front porch together."

After spending a few moments calculating what in the world Alan and I would look and feel like at ages eighty-eight and ninety, rocking on our porch, I knew that nothing could have made the girls happier than hearing those words. No more rental house, no more time split between parents. Mattie, Ali, and Dani could grow up in the security of knowing their parents were working out their relationship, day by day, and would be together for them as long as God gave us on this earth.

The following Sunday was Mother's Day. The girls and I went to church, but Alan chose to stay home. I assumed that he was just too physically and emotionally wrung out to go with us.

But when we returned home from the worship service, the house was full of the aromas of roast beef, mashed potatoes, fresh green beans and corn, buttery yeast rolls, and warm banana pudding. Alan ushered us into the dining room. He had set the table with our best china and crystal, linen napkins, white candles, and an enormous floral arrangement.

"Happy Mother's Day!" he shouted. The older girls laughed and hugged us both, and baby Dani smiled a baby smile.

I was overwhelmed. Alan's thoughtfulness in wanting to make this day special was just one of the many things he did for me in the weeks and months to come—physical acts of kindness to show me the intentions of his heart. He had made a real commitment to change. He was putting the past behind and making our marriage the best that it could be. He had been away long enough to realize that restoring our relationship was worth the effort that it would require.

Today as I look back on our baby steps in rebuilding our marriage, I sometimes think what our lives would be like if we hadn't started over. I realize that not all situations are like ours, and that there are situations where divorce is warranted. But for us, we knew that God was calling us back to our marriage vows, and that He was giving us a fresh start.

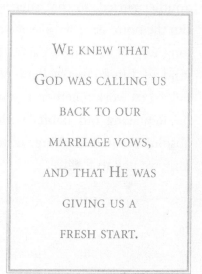

WE KNEW THAT GOD WAS CALLING US BACK TO OUR MARRIAGE VOWS, AND THAT HE WAS GIVING US A FRESH START.

In order to take it, though, we had to do a lot of hard things. I've already mentioned how difficult it was to take off old, well-worn habits that were quite comfortable, and to replace them with new ways of interacting with God and each other. It's hard to get out of old ruts. But we were both committed to doing just that, and it became perversely fun, in a way, to respond to each other in new and different ways.

For example, if we were planning to go out, Alan would ask, "Where do you want to go, Denise? What do you want to do?"

"Oh, Alan, it really doesn't matter, whatever you want to do."

"No!" Alan would groan. "Don't tell me we went through all that therapy for nothing! What do you *really* want to do?"

Then we'd rewind the conversation—"*?od ot tnaw uoy od tahW ?esineD, og ot tnaw uoy od erehW*"—and start over.

"Sorry," I'd say. "Let's see, tonight I *really* want to go eat some sushi!"

As you may know from his music, Alan prefers his sushi Southern-fried, so that suggestion wouldn't go over very well. But the point is, as hard as it was to actually change our decades-long way of relating—particularly on little things—it was also kind of fun to make light of our past dysfunctions. Humor helped us work together to start new habits.

Replacing old habits with new ones was tough. But the absolutely toughest thing we had to do was also the most important: we had to forgive.

A HARD ROAD

Oh, for the wonderful love He has promised,
Promised for you and for me.
Though we have sinned He has mercy and pardon,
Pardon for you and for me.

Will L. Thompson, "Softly and Tenderly"

. . . life was changed, disassembled, rearranged
We came together, fell apart
And broke each other's hearts
Remember when

Remember when the sound of little feet
was the music
We danced to week to week
Brought back the love, we found trust
Vowed we'd never give it up
Remember when

Alan Jackson, "Remember When"

In order to have a true fresh start, we had to rebuild trust. For, of course, the worst blow to our marriage had not been bad habits or codependency or my indecisiveness. The deepest wound had been the destruction of trust because of betrayal in our relationship. Alan had not been faithful. And he had covered it up.

By this point, as ugly and painful as it was, he had confessed everything. And as hard as the truth was for me to accept, it was the missing piece of the puzzle. I had felt for a while that something was different, of course, but now Alan put it all together for me. Now I knew why, after all these years, he had wanted to actually separate and go our different ways.

It felt so strange and awful. On one hand he was so familiar to me, the man he'd always been . . . but on the other hand it was like he was a different person altogether. I would look at his face, his eyes, his hands, and think, *How could the man I'd known and loved all these years, with whom I'd had three children, have had this hidden part of his life I knew nothing about?*

I realize, of course, that infidelity happens every day. Plenty of people, celebrities and otherwise, break their marriage vows. But, like most spouses, I never thought that it could happen to *me*. I was so full of anger, shame, and pain that I hardly knew which way to turn.

But God had entered into this sad story. He had brought me a long way. He was working in Alan as well, bringing him back to Himself and also to me. And as Alan confessed everything, it was a huge relief for him. It felt so freeing to no longer have secrets he was trying to hide. It was actually liberating to confess his wrongdoings, and to ask for my forgiveness.

I was thankful, in a really painful way, that he had brought it all out in the open. I appreciated that he was courageous enough to tell all and ask for my pardon. After all, if he wasn't repentant, we weren't going to get anywhere in rebuilding our relationship. By "repentant," I don't mean guilty and miserable. Real repentance is actually freeing; it lifts the burden of guilt. And it's shown not just by words, but by deeds.

Thankfully, as I'll show in a moment, Alan made real changes in behavior that demonstrated his changes in convictions.

WOULD I SMOOTH THINGS OVER IN A SUPERFICIAL WAY, TAKING HIM BACK AND ACTING AS IF ALL WAS WELL, BUT STILL HOLDING ON TO ALAN'S WRONGS LIKE ACES UP MY SLEEVE, TO BE WHIPPED OUT WHENEVER I NEEDED TO TRUMP HIM?

But the first step lay with me, and it was a huge challenge.

Would I really forgive? *Could* I forgive? Or would I smooth things over in a superficial way, taking him back and acting as if all was well, but still holding on to Alan's wrongs like aces up my sleeve, to be whipped out whenever I needed to trump him?

No Denial

My lifelong habit of denial was not going to work in this situation. I couldn't just cover things over and forge ahead, acting like nothing had happened. In order for *me* to be set free, as well as Alan, I had to clearly acknowledge the wrongs he'd done. And then if I wanted to go forward, I had to forgive. There was no escaping it.

I've talked with so many women who can relate to this dilemma. Even if your marriage hasn't gone through a time like this, all of us have been wronged in one way or another. We've all been hurt by others, whether our spouses, friends, relatives, acquaintances, grown children, employers, whomever. But when we hold on to bitterness and resentment, it doesn't really injure the ones who wronged us. It hurts *us*. And it can absolutely destroy us.

There's no one-size-fits-all kind of answer or formula for forgiveness. For each of us, the struggle will be individual. But what I found, in the long run, was that forgiveness was the key to real freedom in my life. It unlocked all kinds of new blessings.

Of course when I found myself confronted with the need to forgive Alan, I couldn't see ahead to the good things that forgiveness would bring in my future. Nor could I relate to what other people had done or not done in similar situations.

All I knew was that if I was really going to do everything that I could do to make my marriage work, I had to forgive completely. I felt anxious and pained by the whole process, but I also felt a strong sense of God's presence. I really knew that *He* was always faithful, even if human relationships weren't. I read in the

New Testament, "Do not be anxious about anything, but in everything, by prayer and petition, with thanksgiving, present your requests to God. And the peace of God, which transcends all understanding, will guard your hearts and your minds in Christ Jesus."[1]

I desperately wanted that supernatural peace of God!

So I tried to do what those verses said, step by step. I prayed, pouring out my concerns to God. I thanked Him for the fact that I could even have a relationship with Him. I asked Him to do things in my heart that I just could not do on my own. I asked Him to erase pictures in my mind that tortured me. I asked Him to free me from rage. And I prayed that He would help me to be the loving, forgiving wife that I wanted to be.

I knew I could not be that person through my own good intentions or willpower. I wasn't strong enough. But God was strong enough to do miracles in me, starting with giving me His peace right in the midst of the pain of Alan's betrayal. And He kept the miracles coming, giving me what I needed to be able to forgive the wrongs done to me.

Tenderized

Oddly enough, the more I prayed, the more tender my hard heart became. Something very strange started to happen. I was struck by the wrongs *I* had done and motivated to humbly ask Alan for forgiveness for how I had hurt him.

This was *way* beyond my normal way of thinking. It happened because God brought a familiar part of Scripture to life for me in a new way. In the Sermon on the Mount, Jesus said that if you even *look* at someone lustfully, you have committed adultery in your heart.

I'd heard that all my life, but I'd never felt convicted about it before. Now, though, I realized that if I'd felt any moral superiority over Alan because I'd never actually *committed* adultery, Christ's words certainly nixed that. I, too, had been tempted. During my flying career and other times, men had shown all kinds of interest in me. I'd had opportunities to respond to that attention. I'd never given in. But I'd had thoughts and daydreams that failed Christ's tough standard.

Of course there's a big difference in the *consequences* of actual adultery versus impurity or unfaithfulness in one's thought life. But my ability to forgive Alan had a lot to do with realizing that I, too, was in need of forgiveness for a wandering heart and a lack of focused love and communication in my marriage.

As I thought about all this, parts of the Bible came alive for me like never before. For example, I love the story in the New Testament of the woman who came to see Jesus one night when He was having dinner at the home of a religious leader. This woman had "lived a sinful life,"[2] the Bible says. She was determined to see Jesus, and she got into the courtyard where He was dining. She washed His feet with her tears, wiped them with her hair, and put perfume on them.

That all sounds quite strange to us. But in Jesus' day, since people wore sandals, and their feet became quite dusty from the unpaved roads, house servants would normally wash guests' feet, using a basin of water, and wipe them with a clean towel.

But this woman did much more. She *kissed* Jesus' feet. She wet them with her tears. She dried them with her long hair and anointed them with perfume. She gave everything she had to show Him how sorry she was for her former lifestyle . . . and how much she loved Jesus.

The religious leaders were absolutely horrified. This was not proper.

So Jesus told them a story. Say that you have two people who have borrowed money, He said. One owes a million dollars to a moneylender; the other owes a hundred. Neither one can pay him back. So the lender forgives both debts, canceling them out.

Which person will love the lender more? Jesus asks.

The one whose debt was bigger and was forgiven more, says the host.

Exactly, says Jesus. *Those who are forgiven a lot love a lot.* "But he who has been forgiven little loves little."[3]

As I thought about what forgiveness really meant in my own life, I realized that the same was true for me. If I could begin to see how big and revolting my sins really were in God's eyes, and yet how He had wiped out every single one of them, then I'd have a big love for Him.

The Psalms told me that God's love for me was bigger than I could imagine, "as high as the heavens are above the earth," and that He had removed my sins "as far as the east is from the west."[4] It's absolutely enormous: I couldn't fathom how high God's love was, nor how wide was His pardon of my sins.

But out of the overflowing gratitude of realizing that *I'd* been totally forgiven, I could follow Jesus' lead and forgive the debts of others who owed me. "Be kind and compassionate to one another, forgiving each other, just as in Christ God forgave you," Ephesians 4:32 says.

Now that I had some big forgiving to do, and I had a new sense of God's forgiveness of *me*, I could really roll up my sleeves and put that Scripture into practice. It wasn't just a dry old Bible verse. It was a flexible, freeing life principle.[5]

Life out of Death

As I began to understand this, one of my watershed moments came, fittingly, on Easter. As the girls and I drove to church on Easter, during the time that Alan and I were still separated, I was thinking about the message that I would hear, like so many Easters before. Christ died to pay the punishment for human sin, so that the wrongdoings of those who believed in Him would be forgiven. It was a truth I'd grown up believing, but had taken for granted in my everyday life.

But on this Resurrection morning, with new life and fresh blossoms bursting forth all around me, the Holy Spirit seemed to speak to me like never before. It was as if Christ was saying to me, "Denise, I died for all of your sins, the ones in your past and the ones that you have not yet committed, so that you could be forgiven for all of them. I loved you enough to do that for you. Even before you were born, I chose to die for you so that we could have an intimate, loving relationship forever! With My help, you can do the same for Alan. If you will follow My example, I will bless your marriage and make it new."

When I arrived at church, every word of the sermon that day

seemed to hinge on one thing—my willingness to forgive Alan, so that real restoration, emotional closeness, and freedom could be ours.

Forgiveness was the first step in rebuilding our marriage. But in order to go forward, day by day, we also had to rebuild trust—and forgiveness and trust are two different things.

Thanks to what God was doing inside of me, I was able to forgive Alan. Though on a much smaller scale, of course, my forgiveness was a copy of Jesus' forgiveness of me. Forgiveness is a grace that is freely given to the offender by the one who's been offended. It's a gift.

But *trust* has to be earned. Rebuilding it takes

> MY FORGIVENESS OF ALAN DIDN'T MEAN THAT I WAS BLIND, OR HAD MY HEAD STUCK IN THE SAND. AS WE MOVED FORWARD, I DIDN'T JUST WANT NICE WORDS. I WANTED TO SEE REAL CHANGES IN WHAT ALAN DID.

changed behaviors continued over time. My forgiveness of Alan didn't mean that I was blind, or had my head stuck in the sand. As we moved forward, I didn't just want nice words. I wanted to see real changes in what Alan did. I wanted to see different actions, so I could reasonably expect different outcomes.

Thankfully, we were on the same page. He not only *told* me

that he wanted to save and restore our marriage. He *showed* me, in tangible ways, humbly doing whatever he could to demonstrate that he was willing to live transparently. No secrets.

It was hard work, but Alan has never been one to be afraid of working hard. For one thing, he was very sensitive to how I was feeling. As I worked through everything going on inside of me, I had a lot of anger, tears, and frustration. If I heard about someone who'd been unfaithful in his marriage, or if there was an adulterous character in a movie we were watching, I'd blow up.

"It's your fault that I react this way!" I'd yell at him. And the good thing was, Alan would not only let me vent, but he also really heard my pain. He put himself as best he could in my shoes, trying to understand and empathize with the thunderstorm of emotions that were flooding the dry ground inside of me.

He also made changes in his professional life. In terms of his concerts and the many temptations that can come with life on the road, he started flying to every engagement, rather than taking the tour bus. He called me and our children all the time, giving short accounts of where he was and what he was doing. There was never a time when I couldn't get him to answer his cell phone when I called, as there had been before. And almost without exception, he flew home after every show rather than staying out on the road. He broke off relationships with people whose influence might negatively affect his new commitment.

No one is perfect. But as much as Alan's unfaithfulness had hurt me, his willingness to change his behaviors and work hard to make a new start impressed me. After all, he could have taken an easy road. He was a superstar; it would have been easy to go off and hang out with people who would tell him he was just perfect, or whatever he might have wanted to hear. And he certainly would have had thousands of choices!

But Alan had made a new commitment to himself and to our marriage. We had gone through many wonderful seasons and also many times when things weren't all they could be between us. But at this point Alan had figured out who he was and who he wanted to be, and he was careful to avoid stumbling blocks that would hinder his decision.

Daily Restoration

As we made our way through this tender time of rebuilding our marriage, we really believed that our slates had been wiped clean, that it was a fresh start. But we've also had to keep working at these principles. We've had to realize and practice the truth that real biblical forgiveness is an ongoing, daily process. As long as we live, we will have to face the reality of our dark side, what the Bible calls our sin nature.

I've realized this more and more in my daily prayer time. The Bible says, "If we claim to be without sin, we deceive ourselves and the truth is not in us. If we confess our sins, [Jesus] is faithful and just and will forgive us our sins and purify us from all unrighteousness. If we claim we have not sinned, we make him out to be a liar and his word has no place in our lives."[6]

When I'm sitting with our little dog in the morning, my prayer journal in my lap and a cup of coffee in my hand, I've found it really helpful to write down anything from the previous day that I need forgiveness for. God will often prompt me to remember something that I hadn't even been thinking about: talking abruptly or impatiently with someone, hurting someone's feelings, not spending time with one of our girls when she needed me, being full of pride instead of humility, putting my needs and wishes before others . . . the list goes on and on.

But each day, I know that God hears my prayers! He knows my heart. He's changing me, day by day. He loves me, and as I confess my sins and shortcomings, He forgives them freely and restores our relationship.

Incredible!

Though Alan and I are obviously both sinful humans, the same principle applies in our relationship. We try to address hurts and misunderstandings every day as they occur, so that they don't drive a wedge between us. I no longer live in the denial mode, pretending that everything is just fine when it isn't.

And unlike years ago, now we rarely go to bed with unresolved anger or hurts. Every night Alan closes up the house and makes sure all the doors are locked while I go upstairs and lie down with Dani for a while. I rub her back and pray with her while Alan putters around downstairs.

Then I go to Mattie's and Ali's rooms and visit with each of them for a few minutes. Telling my girls that I love them is a given—as automatic as brushing my teeth. I try to remember to praise them for specific accomplishments, and to encourage them as I feel they need it. But more than anything, I try to help them understand that they are loved for who they are—children of God—not because of anything that they have done.

Each of these girls God has given us is unique. Mattie is a quiet achiever, while Ali is an outgoing girl who loves the spotlight . . . kind of like how I was at her age! Dani is a mixture of the two. When Ali started playing on a soccer team, she was on a mixed team with boys. In any fast-break situation, she'd get the ball from any guy she needed to—even if he was on her team—and take it down the field, until we explained to her that you don't steal the ball from your own teammates.

When Ali was about four years old, she and I had a conflict about something. Later, as I was looking out the window toward the pastures at the back of our property, I saw a small person toting a pink, fake-fur suitcase, striding along indignantly. Ali was running away from home. I called our nanny, who lived in the barn apartment at the time, and told her to be ready for one very independently minded visitor!

During our nightly routine, while I'm praying with each of our wonderful girls, Alan sets up the coffee to brew for the next morning so it will be ready when we wake up, groggy and in need of caffeine. Sometimes he finds my grocery and to-do lists and adds little reminders to them, subtle hints like "Do something nice for Alan today." Then he tends to the smallest and highest-maintenance of our pets, Miss Coco Chanel. (Our mutt, Buddy, and our Westie, Opie, are manly dogs that sleep in the garage.)

Alan plugs in Coco's bed warmer, takes the barrette out of her silky hair, and tucks her tiny self into her little pink bed in the laundry room. (I often wonder what Alan's tough-guy fans would think if they could see him so carefully nurturing this four-pound Yorkie who wears clothes!)

Then he comes upstairs, he kisses each of the girls good night, and we climb into our big bed. I lie with my head on his shoulder, my arm wrapped around him and his enveloping me, snuggling in the same way that we've lain down to go to sleep all these long years of our marriage. Even if we've hardly seen each other during the day, we so easily reconnect during these private minutes together. It's a time when we both can shut out the pressures and stresses of our day and remember that no matter what has gone on, all is well. We laugh a little, talk about the day, and try to make sure there's no tension between us, apologizing if we had any misunderstandings. By that time we're both usually so tired that we are quite anxious to forgive each other, so we can go to sleep!

This isn't rocket science. It's just a simple habit that we've tried to develop with each other. As we've practiced it, we've found that we go to sleep easier, sleep better, and wake up refreshed and recommitted to each other. Small hurts left unaddressed no longer smolder into large issues that wreak havoc on our relationship.

This kind of housekeeping in our relationship is pretty simple, really. It just follows the basic principle our mothers always told us when we were growing up: you have to take out the trash every single day . . . or it starts to stink.

Chapter 19

MAKING NEW VOWS

⚜

Instead of their shame
my people will receive a double portion,
and instead of disgrace
they will rejoice in their inheritance;
and so they will inherit a double portion in their land,
and everlasting joy will be theirs.

Isaiah 61:7

As Alan and I were rebuilding our relationship in those early days after our separation, we weren't alone. As I've said, friends were praying for us, supporting us, wanting the best for us. Our friend Bobbie not only prayed for us every day; she even wrote down her prayers in a journal. One morning Bobbie sipped her coffee and read Psalm 32. "God Will Provide Songs of Victory," she wrote as she jotted down some of the words of the Psalm.

"Blessed is he whose transgressions are forgiven . . . let everyone who is godly pray to you while you may be found. . . . You are my hiding place, you will protect me from trouble and surround me with songs of deliverance."

Bobbie thought about how King David, who wrote so many of the Psalms, was a musician. She thought about how David's "lyrics" could connect with Alan in a special way since they were both songwriters.

"Lord," Bobbie wrote in her prayer journal, "I pray that Alan will find joy in Your presence and forgiveness, just like David . . . I pray that Denise will pray to You and You will be found . . . that You will be her hiding place and protect Alan, Denise, Mattie, Ali, and Dani from trouble! I pray that Alan will write songs of victory, and that You would surround his family with deliverance and Your abiding love. May they rejoice in the Lord and be glad! May they sing with upright hearts!"

Years later, the last part of Bobbie's sincere prayer came true in ways I couldn't have imagined when Alan and I were gingerly putting our marriage back together.

A Brand-New Marriage

Once it seemed like our marriage actually might last, I told Alan that I wanted visible reminders of the new commitment that was written in our hearts. "We've had a fresh start," I said. "I want a ceremony where other people can see us making this new commitment. I don't want to look down at my wedding ring and remember vows that were broken. And I don't want our anniversary to be a reminder of that either. I want it to be a day of renewal and recommitment."

Our old rings were yellow gold, bought when we were just eighteen and twenty, from the old jewelry store on Jackson Street in Newnan, where I had worked as a teenager. On our long-ago wedding-day morning, Alan had realized that his ring was too big, and he didn't want to lose it. So my sister, Jane, had to run out to the jeweler to have it resized just before the ceremony.

Almost nineteen years later, we had almost lost not our rings, but our marriage. But now it was being restored. And now we weren't kids anymore. Our love had been tested sorely by pain, assaulted by our own selfishness and pride, refined by the cleansing fire of God's love and forgiveness.

To commemorate all this, we had new rings made of platinum. One of the most treasured elements on the planet, platinum is more precious than gold or silver. It is rarer. It is more durable.

We believed, by God's grace, that we'd been refined by difficulties, purified, and given the gift of a new, platinum marriage. Not that Alan or I had become so

> OUR NEW RINGS
> WERE A SYMBOL
> OF THE COMMITMENT
> WE WERE NOW
> WILLING TO MAKE,
> A COMMITMENT TO
> A DEEP, TRUE LOVE
> THAT HAD ITS ROOTS
> IN THE LOVE AND
> AMAZING GRACE
> OF GOD.

unusual or refined. Far from it. Our new marriage wasn't all about us, as though if we tried hard enough, our union would be shiny and perfect from that day forward.

But we had a new view of marriage as a treasured *gift* that is far more precious than appearances, mind games, cheap pleasures, or hanging on to pride and control. Our new rings were a symbol of the commitment we were now willing to make, a commitment to a deep, true love that had its roots in the love and amazing grace of God.

Our anniversary was on a weekday, and we scheduled our little service for the midmorning. Our friend and nanny, Mary, came with us to the small chapel at Nashville's First Presbyterian Church with baby Dani. Mattie and Ali were in their school clothes. Robert Wolgemuth, my friend and Sunday school teacher, led the ceremony. His wife, Bobbie, who had prayed so fervently for us, was also there to share in the celebration, as was Jane from the Bible study, and her husband, Tom. Alan's manager at the time, Chip Peay, and his wife at the time, Norma Jane, came as well.

I wore a simple, long dress in a deep wine color. My G.I. Jane hair was still growing out, and it was a wonderful (if superficial) affirmation of Alan's deep and abiding love that Alan was remarrying me, for better or for worse, long-haired or crew cut, though we didn't quite have that written into our vows.

A Future and a Hope

Robert opened the service with Scripture passages, including one of my very favorites, a covenant promise from God that says:

"I will come and do for you all the good things I have promised, and I will bring you home again. For I know the plans I have for you," says the LORD. "They are plans for good and not for disaster, to give you a future and a hope. In those days when you pray, I will listen. If you look for me in earnest, you will find me."[1]

Never before had I so strongly realized the truth of these verses. The Lord had heard my petitions to Him and restored my marriage. He had literally brought Alan home again. He had planned my future before the beginning of time—a future of hope. He took our brokenness and sinfulness and actually brought good out of it. When I called out to Him in desperation, He was faithful to make Himself known to me.

I thought back over the years to the dimly lit church in Newnan on the evening of our first wedding, and how nervous and excited I was. I had loved Alan, as much as I understood about love, but like most other young brides on the planet, I had only the foggiest idea about what was ahead.

As our story unfolded over time, we made it through many chapters full of things both good and bad . . . college, my flying career, pursuing Alan's music dreams, children, failure, success, wealth, and fame. All along the way, it wasn't necessarily any of those *outside* forces that dictated whether our marriage would succeed or fail. Sure, celebrity had brought strange pressures to our union. In a completely different way, our time apart when I was a flight attendant had also stressed us. But, again, it wasn't the power of any external situations or temptations that would determine if we'd stay true. It was the strength of our innermost convictions.

That's why at our 1998 service Alan chose to sing the very same song he'd sung at our ceremony in 1979. It had been true back then, but now we understood its reality far better. As I stood with him and the few close friends around us, watching his fine hands strum his guitar and hearing his smooth baritone sing the words, it really was a brand-new start. Now we were founded on a better foundation, and he was affirming his commitment toward that end.

That's the Way
Pat Terry

With this ring I thee wed
And I give to you my life
Mine is yours and yours is mine
And we can live that way forever
With this kiss we will seal
That we now are man and wife
Two in one, one in two
That's the way it's got to be

With this love, we can live
But we can't keep it to ourselves
He is mine, and He is yours
And we can live our lives in telling
I give my heart, I give my soul
I give you all my worldly goods
Two in one, one in two
That's the way it's got to be

I will cling to you, you will cling to me
And in the shadow of the cross

We'll live on bended knee
With this prayer I commit
That we both become as one
He in us and we in Him
Saying vows to one another
Hold them fast in your heart
'Til the day we see the Son
Two in one, one in two
That's the way it's go to be[2]

Two in one, and one in two. We had learned that Alan and I couldn't be truly one by the power of our own commitment. We could only be truly, intimately linked if we were both dependent on God. We could only be one *in Him.* It was supernatural . . . the sense that flawed human beings are able, because of grace, to have peace with God . . . and consequently live in peace with one another.

Beginning Again

Tears filled my eyes as I remembered how I had felt on this day just one year earlier.

On that prior gray December anniversary, I had been lost, so full of fear and anger that I could not imagine ever feeling joyful again. I had also been full of shame. I felt rejected, exposed, and humiliated by Alan's defection.

I had also felt, way down deep, that it was all my fault. I knew that wasn't true. But it's hard for your intellect to win an argument over your feelings, especially when something bad is happening.

My feelings had told me that our separation wouldn't have happened if I had just been a little better. Maybe if I had been thinner, smarter, younger, more beautiful, more confident, more fit, funnier, more adventurous, more *whatever*, then Alan wouldn't have strayed. Maybe if I hadn't made stupid mistakes, or perhaps if I had not been selfish, needy, or clingy . . . maybe then I'd be okay. In my shame, it was all about me—my faults, my deficiencies, ways in which I didn't meet a perfect standard.

Many women struggle with this type of thinking. You don't have to have a celebrity husband to feel such humiliation when he leaves. Shame is an equal-opportunity adversary.

Some of us struggle with it because of traumatic events in our past. Many of us feel shame because of a lifelong feeling that we just don't measure up, and we'll go to any extent of denial to cover it over, because *it hurts*. I recently read a magazine article about shame in which the author wrote, "Avoiding humiliation was practically my religion."[3]

She went on to say she eventually learned that "my level of shame was always under my own control, that I would endure exactly as much humiliation as I consented to feel, and that instead of tolerating this awful feeling, I could simply dispense with it."[4]

This is admirable. But I had no idea how to "simply dispense" with shame. I didn't know how to exert enough willpower to get rid of it by myself. It had to be taken away by Someone who had a lot more power than I did.

This is where my new relationship with God worked another miracle. As I learned more about Him with my head and experienced His love with my heart, I was absolutely overwhelmed. His love was so big that it crowded out my shame. For a lifetime,

I'd tried to be "good enough" . . . good enough to merit my father's love, good enough to make Alan proud, good enough to be considered a "good Christian."

Now I knew that I simply *couldn't* be good enough. What a relief to cheerfully admit my inadequacy! On my own, I could never be in a relationship with a perfect, holy God. But Jesus was good enough. Perfectly good. And because of His death on the cross, in my place, for my sins, God credited Christ's perfect righteousness to my account. My debt was paid in full. Cancelled.

As I said earlier, like anyone who was raised in the South and grew up in church, I'd known *about* this all my life. But I didn't really know that it had the power to take away my shame. I didn't discover this until I hit difficult times in my marriage and felt broken into little pieces, raw and exposed.

Then I read in the New Testament, "Let us fix our eyes on Jesus, the author and perfecter of our faith, who for the joy set before him endured the cross, *scorning its shame,* and sat down at the right hand of the throne of God."[5] Jesus took all my sins on the cross. He scorned their shame—and He obliterated shame's power in my life.

So I didn't have to get rid of my shame by the power of positive thinking, like trying to lift a weight that my muscles simply could not budge. No. That weight was lifted from me, freeing me and leaving me lighter than air.

God's love for me was like a cleansing flood, washing away the sad little rags of shame. I was freed from the need to try to be "good enough" to earn anyone's favor. I knew I was loved with an everlasting love simply because of Jesus.

So now, on this December afternoon of 1998, a year after my

cold winter of despair, I had found a new relationship with God . . . and He had made possible a new relationship with Alan. God had taken away my shame and blessed me with a "double portion," as the Old Testament puts it, with "everlasting joy" for this life and the next.

I couldn't believe it.

After Alan and I said our new vows to each other, Robert asked if there was anything else Alan would like to say. Alan talked about how our new platinum rings, like our new marriage, were stronger and more precious than the gold rings we had worn for nineteen years. He humbly made a promise to me in front of our children and our friends to be the man, and the husband, that God wanted him to be.

Then Robert gave us a closing blessing:

> And now, may the God of all grace, forgiveness and restoration
>   guard your hearts and minds.
> May His tangible love continue for you, Alan and Denise,
> for your children and for your children's children.
> May His wisdom direct your decisions.
> May His Holy Spirit guide your emotions.
> May His Word lead your way.
> May His blessing be abundant.
> May His forgiveness and grace give you freedom and creativity.
> May His peace give you assurance and comfort.
> And may His lavishness bring renewed celebration, today
>   and forevermore.
> Those whom God has joined together, let no one ever separate!
> Amen!

Chapter 20

A WORK IN PROGRESS

✧

I even asked the Lord to try to help me:
He looked down from Heaven, said to tell you please;
Just be patient, I'm a work in progress.

Alan Jackson, "Work in Progress"

He who began a good work in you
will carry it on to completion until the day of Christ Jesus.

Philippians 1:6, the Apostle Paul

would love to say that after Alan and I renewed our vows, we were instantly changed into perfect Christians and the perfect couple. It would be great if life was like those extreme-makeover shows on TV, where people are rejuvenated into ideal versions of themselves, what they've always wanted to be.

But lasting transformation takes a lot longer than an hour-long TV show, or the amount of time it takes for plastic surgery

179

to heal. Reality can be disturbing: I've come to realize that life's journey isn't a quick transformational spin, but a long, hard trek of slow growth in an upward direction. Spiritually speaking, sanctification, or becoming more like Jesus, is a lifelong process.

Growth in human relationships is the same way. In our committed-but-not-perfect marriage, Alan and I get up every morning and take each day as it comes, with a renewed pledge to each other and to Christ. We know our progress will be slow . . . but we're moving in the right direction.

Big Hair, Big Fun

One of the unexpected benefits of this may sound superficial, but it's not. I've found that as Alan and I are at ease in our relationship with each other because of God's peace in our lives, we laugh a lot more. Our relationship is a lot more fun. We're free!

One weekend recently, we were staying at a friend of a friend's lake home. The owners were not there, but they had pulled out all the stops to make us comfortable in their absence.

There were fresh flower arrangements in every room. There were gift baskets full of fruit, chocolates, and fine wines. The kitchen was fully stocked with just about anything we could have wanted. It was incredible. No hotel in the world could have given more care to make us feel comfortable.

The first evening we were there, we'd made reservations at a nice restaurant that our friends had recommended. I went into the luxurious master bath and took a long, hot shower, enjoying the designer soaps, shampoos, and gels our hosts had left for us.

I wrapped myself in an enormous, fluffy towel, put on my makeup, and then got ready to do my hair. In order for it to look full and smooth, I'd have to blow it dry with a round brush and a strong hair dryer. The bathroom was stocked with curling irons, ceramic straighteners, everything. Humming, I opened drawers, searching for what I needed. I knew it was right there somewhere.

No hair dryer.

There were about six other fully stocked bathrooms in this lovely home. Still wearing my towel, I called to Alan. He was already dressed and ready to go.

"Honey," I said sweetly, "can you check the other bathrooms and find me a hair dryer?"

"Sure," he said. He went down the hall, and I could hear him opening drawers and cabinets.

He came back. "There's no hair dryer anywhere," he said.

> A moment later, the bathroom door burst open, and Alan strode in, an enormous leaf blower in his arms. He flipped it on, and a tornado of air blasted through the bathroom. Alan looked like someone from *The Texas Chainsaw Massacre*.

I was already envisioning my hair, wet and plastered to my head, drying in pathetic clumps. I clenched my teeth and smiled.

"This house has absolutely everything," I said. "There *has* to be a hair dryer somewhere. And you *have to* find it!"

Alan knew not to mess with me when I was having hair issues. He skedaddled away to search some more.

A few minutes later I heard a triumphant shout from the direction of the garage.

"Nisey!" Alan called. "I found one!"

Thank goodness, I thought.

A moment later, the bathroom door burst open and Alan strode in, an enormous leaf blower in his arms. He flipped it on, and a tornado of air blasted through the bathroom. Tissues flew everywhere. Alan looked like someone from *The Texas Chainsaw Massacre.*

But I wasn't going to question God's provision.

"Okay!" I shouted over the din as my hair whipped in the hurricane-force wind. "You hold it steady, and just move it up and down when I tell you!"

Needless to say, when we finally arrived at the restaurant, I had very *big* hair. But it was dry.

Finishing the Race

Even as Alan has supported me in hair issues, I've tried to affirm my love for him by entering into his interests.

Ever since I met my husband, he's been crazy about cars. His father was a mechanic, and Alan inherited his love of vehicles and his habit of constantly buying, trading, fixing, and selling cars, boats, you name it. Once when Alan was a young boy, his daddy went to a flea market and came home with a broken street sweeper. This was not on his mother's shopping list. It had big suction vents, rotating black brushes, and wide tires. Daddy Gene got it running, and Alan remembers riding up and down his driveway in Georgia, sweeping the hard dirt till it shone.

Alan hasn't brought home any street sweepers lately, but in the interest of marital unity, I've tried to participate in his love of cars. A few years ago he wanted to do a big car rally, a four-day drive called the New England 1000. I joined right in. The idea was for each team to drive preplanned routes through the beautiful countryside, keeping careful track of mileage, timing, and our oil gauges. We were to check in at designated stops throughout the day and have our official time logged by the rally officials. Alan, of course, was our team driver, and I was the official navigator, which meant I had to read the map and keep us going in the right direction.

WE STOPPED FOR LUNCH, CHANGED INTO OUR WATERPROOF JUMP-SUITS IN THE REST-ROOM, AND CAME OUT LOOKING LIKE NINJAS.

We drove a blue AC Cobra, a serious two-seater race car with no top and no windows. We had brought matching black full-body jumpsuits in case of rain, full-face helmets, a stopwatch, a notebook, directions, and pit-stop instructions. We were locked, loaded, and ready to do our 250 miles per day.

All was well until the rain began. At first it just drizzled, but then the clouds rolled in, and a heavy, cold, drenching downpour settled down on the Northeast, centered right above our car. We stopped for lunch, changed into our waterproof jumpsuits in the restroom, and came out looking like ninjas.

As the rain continued, I became less and less tolerant of my husband's beloved hobby. The little windshield had wipers, but I had to use a chamois every other minute to wipe down the inside of the windshield so Alan could see. At first I squeezed it outside the car, but then I realized it really didn't matter. Our little blue Cobra was filling up like a leaky rowboat.

Then my jumpsuit decided to stop being waterproof. Like the car, it began to gradually fill with rainwater. I felt like I was sitting in a wet diaper. For hours. My hair was plastered to my cold head, I could not feel my fingers, and by the time we finally pulled up to our lodging for that evening, I was so cold I could barely speak.

When we went inside, I was absolutely flabbergasted to discover that *everyone else* in the entire rally had given up because of the rain. They had skipped the meandering, scenic route and had come directly to the hotel many hours earlier. They were warm and dry, sitting by a roaring fire. Alan and I—who both looked like refugees from Waterworld—were the only participants who had driven the entire route for the day—without any cover!

Furious, I rushed into the hotel room, stripped off my sopping suit, and stood in the hot shower for about an hour. By the time I emerged, pink and gently wrinkled like a prune, I was actually able to be civil to my husband again.

At the end of the week, after the thousandth mile, the rally people had a big closing banquet. As awards were handed out, Alan and I were surprised when our names were called. "And to Alan and Denise Jackson," the emcee said, "we present the Good Sport Award, for staying out in the rain and not giving up when everyone else did!"

Everyone laughed, and I stood up. "Thank you so much," I said. "I'd just like to add that car rallies are not my usual thing; I did this for my husband. And I want you all to know that I will be receiving a very large piece of jewelry from Big Al when I get home!"

I was kidding, of course, and everyone roared with laughter. It was a light moment . . . but when I thought about it later, I realized that crazy road rally was in some ways a picture of what God had allowed Alan and me to do in our marriage. It had been tough and uncomfortable, but we hadn't bailed out. We had stuck together. We were both determined enough—or maybe I should say stubborn enough—to stay the course.

And by God's grace, we plan to finish the race!

Chapter 21

WHAT REALLY MATTERS

❧

Did you weep for the children
Who lost their dear loved ones
And pray for the ones who don't know
Did you rejoice for the people who walked from the rubble
And sob for the ones left below

Did you burst out in pride
For the red white and blue
The heroes who died just doing what they do
Did you look up to heaven for some kind of answer
And look at yourself to what really matters

I'm just a singer of simple songs
I'm not a real political man
I watch CNN but I'm not sure I can tell you
The difference in Iraq and Iran
But I know Jesus and I talk to God
And I remember this from when I was young
Faith hope and love are some good things he gave us
And the greatest is love

Alan Jackson,
"Where Were You? (When the World Stopped Turning)"

Now we see but a poor reflection as in a mirror; then we shall see
face to face. Now I know in part; then I shall know fully,
even as I am fully known.
And now these three remain: faith, hope and love.
But the greatest of these is love.

1 Corinthians 13:12–13

On the morning of September 11, 2001, Alan was at home. I was at my Tuesday morning Bible study. The children were at school. When I heard the news, I rushed home, and like everyone else in the country, Alan and I stood in front of the television, our hands over our mouths, tears in our eyes.

A few weeks after that terrible day, Alan woke in the middle of the night. The melody and a few lines of a song were running through his mind. He crept downstairs to his office and sang into his little hand-held voice recorder, worried that if he waited until morning, he'd forget it all. Then he came upstairs and quietly slipped back into bed, not realizing that what he had just recorded would touch so many who were suffering from the 9/11 tragedies.

The next morning he finished writing the song. It was called "Where Were You? (When the World Stopped Turning)," and it eventually went to the top of not just the country charts, but the general market and pop genres as well. It struck a chord. As *USA Weekend* later reported, "The No. 1 success of 'Where Were You?', which captures a myriad of reactions to the terrorist attacks, has elevated Jackson to a new plateau of fame. People who had never before listened to country music bought his 2.5 million-selling 'Drive' album and came home to the core values of God, country and family that the genre has typically embraced."[1]

For his part, Alan said that he didn't really create the lyrics for "Where Were You?" "God wrote it," he said later. "I just held the pencil."[2]

In some ways Alan is a very complicated person. In other ways, as his song says, he's just a singer of simple songs. His simplicity nailed what many people felt about September 11. It touched many for whom the attacks were not only a horrible catastrophe, but also a wake-up call about what really matters in this life.

> IN SOME WAYS ALAN IS A VERY COMPLICATED PERSON. IN OTHER WAYS, AS HIS SONG SAYS, HE'S JUST A SINGER OF SIMPLE SONGS. HIS SIMPLICITY NAILED WHAT MANY PEOPLE FELT ABOUT SEPTEMBER 11.

The terrorist assaults pierced the hearts of people across America and around the world. They brought everything to a halt for a while. They sifted out unessential things that so often clamor for our attention. They highlighted what was truly important.

God's Story, My Story

Even disasters or losses on a far, far smaller scale than 9/11 can stop us in our tracks. When we sit by the deathbed of a loved one, we cherish our relationship as never before. When Alan's daddy had an aortic aneurysm about six months before September 11, Alan sat helplessly by his hospital bedside. Daddy Gene was bleeding internally, and Alan's heart broke as he watched his father take his last breath, even as his once-strong heartbeat slowed and stopped for good. Alan had realized in a new way just how gentle and decent his daddy had been . . . and he had resolved to be more like him.

And for me, when my brother took his own life, it was like a knife cutting through the clutter in my heart and the complacent comfort of my lifestyle. I began to think about God, faith, and eternity in new ways. When the break came in my marriage to Alan, it woke me up to fundamental changes that I needed to make in my relationship with God.

Recently I read a book by a Christian counselor named Dan Allender. He says some wild things about tragedy and crisis, things that make sense when I think about how God has worked in my life. "The tragedies of life, small and large, carve contours in our character that draw us to a different way of living, one that God intends to both use and transform."[3]

God is writing a story in our lives, Dr. Allender says. Our lives aren't just random, unconnected collections of scenes without meaning. They have purpose, and as we become more and more tuned in to who God is, we can actually participate with Him in the way our story turns out. We can have peace in the plot's strange twists and turns. We can be free from fear of the bad guys. We can shine with God's love and draw other people to see God's good story in their own lives.

Many of us have chapters that we would prefer had never

been written. There are sections of my story that I used to wish I could delete like a computer file. One quick click of the mouse and those chapters would be gone. I just wanted to keep the cheerful parts.

But now I'm beginning to learn that the hard chapters show God's power in a way that the happy ones do not. Brokenness moves my story forward in a way that peaceful times do not. It's in difficulties that I became desperate to really know God, to cry out to Him.

> BROKENNESS MOVES MY STORY FORWARD IN A WAY THAT PEACEFUL TIMES DO NOT. IT'S IN DIFFICULTIES THAT I BECAME DESPERATE TO REALLY KNOW GOD, TO CRY OUT TO HIM.

As Dan Allender says, we only learn to accept and love our story "to the degree that we see the glory that seeps through our most significant shattering. To see that glory, we must enter into and read our tragedies with confidence that they will end better than we could ever imagine."[4]

When everything is going well, we often can't hear God, because the music all around us is turned up too loud. But when the party stops—in those moments of crashing pain, sorrow, and sudden silence—we begin to hear His voice. I've learned that if I listen and lean on His strength, He can help me climb out of the wreckage. As I do, I have new perspectives about what is precious and what is truly important.

Singing with Upright Hearts

The older I get, the more I also see how this pattern of broken-ness and restoration reflects the big picture of God's great story.

The Gospel is all about God coming to earth as a real human being. Jesus walked on dusty roads. He laughed and went on pic-nics. He felt weakness and pain. In the end, He was tortured and executed. In human myths, people are sacrificed for gods . . . but in Christianity, God gave Himself for His people. And out of that ultimate weakness—that "most significant shattering"—came the glory of resurrection. Because Christ's story on earth ended in triumph, we have the assurance that ours will end well, too, if we know Him.

God's story is far stronger than the nicest fairy tales we know. As I've seen in my own life, it unfolds over time, weaving together strands of joy, sorrow, friends' prayers, and God's mys-terious will.

In 2002, CMT (Country Music Television) filmed an hour-long Christmas special featuring Alan's new CD, *Let It Be Christmas*. It was a great opportunity for him to promote the CD, but it also gave him a chance to showcase what he had come to realize really matters, particularly after September 11. The show celebrated family, faith, and the great story of Christmas.

The special received lots of positive feedback, and so the net-work has continued to reair it, year after year. Several Christmases after it was first broadcast, Bobbie Wolgemuth flipped on her TV. Robert and Bobbie had moved to another state, and we'd lost touch with them awhile after Alan and I had renewed our vows. The Wolgemuths hadn't really known how we were doing in terms of recommitment to God and each other. Now they watched this crazy Christmas special and got an insight into what had been going on in the Jackson household.

Wearing a bright red jacket and his trademark Stetson cowboy hat, Alan sang "Santa Claus Is Coming to Town" while Ali and Dani, both dressed in sparkling red elf costumes, danced with a few friends from Ali's dance class. Mattie read the account of the first Christmas from the Gospel of Luke as a guitarist played a beautiful introduction to "Silent Night." The cameras zoomed in on our mothers, who were smiling and clapping with the audience. And at the end of the show, our entire family came onto the stage, our arms around one another, and sang the sweet words to the Christmas song Alan had written for his album:

> Let it be Christmas everywhere
> Let heavenly music fill the air
> Let every heart sing, let every bell ring
> The story of hope and joy and peace
> And let it be Christmas everywhere
> Let heavenly music fill the air
> Let anger and fear and hate disappear
> Let there be love that lasts through the year . . .

Watching the broadcast, Bobbie shook her head in wonder. The words from just one of the many prayers she had prayed for us and written in her prayer journal—four years earlier—popped into her mind.

"I pray that Alan will write songs of victory," she had written back in 1998. "And that You would surround his family with deliverance and Your abiding love. May they rejoice in the Lord and be glad! May they sing with upright hearts!"

And there we were, courtesy of Bobbie's TV screen. We weren't perfect, but we were upright, rejoicing in the Lord and being glad. And we were singing with all our hearts. Bobbie could tell that her prayer for us had been answered. She could see that God was continuing to unfold His great story—the story, as Alan's song put it, of "hope and joy and peace," and "love that lasts through the years"—in our lives.

Chapter 22

ROOTS

❦

Remain in me, and I will remain in you.
No branch can bear fruit by itself; it must remain in the vine.
Neither can you bear fruit unless you remain in me.
I am the vine; you are the branches.
If a man remains in me and I in him, he will bear much fruit;
apart from me you can do nothing.

John 15:4–5

got the call on a Wednesday afternoon in June 2005.

"Daddy fell," my sister Jane said. "He broke his leg. I think you'd better come to Newnan."

My father was ninety-one years old. Obviously, I knew that he wasn't going to be with us forever . . . but still, he had come through three major surgeries in the past three years, and I assumed he'd come through this medical challenge as well. I didn't realize that the time had come to say good-bye.

I took care of some arrangements and got to Newnan the following morning. Daddy was in intensive care in the hospital there, sedated and dozing. My mother and sister were in the room with him, and my mama's face was weary with worry. At eighty-four, she had been by his side, in sickness and in health, for the sixty-seven years of their married life.

"Mother," I said, "let me take you out to lunch while Daddy's sleeping. You need a little break from being in the hospital room."

But my mother didn't want to go to lunch with me. She told me she'd go instead with one of my dad's caregivers, who was also a family friend. That seemed strange to me.

"Okay," I said, teasing her. "If you love Janna more than me, that's just fine."

They left . . . and my mother's uncharacteristic "rejection" of my lunch companionship gave me the gift of private time with my father—time that I would never have again.

Fishing in Heaven

I pulled the hard hospital chair close to his narrow bed. I sat with him for hours, holding his hand. I watched his chest rise and fall with each shallow breath. I thought about when I was a little girl and I'd ride on his strong back, laughing, while he galloped across our family room like a pony.

The nurses brought his lunch, and Daddy roused a little. I gently scooped tiny spoonfuls of mashed potatoes and brought them to his lips, but he had a hard time swallowing. I tried to help him sip apple juice through a straw, guiding him as tenderly as he had once tended me as a child.

He dozed on and off throughout the afternoon, then mumbled to me through the oxygen mask that covered his nose and mouth.

"Nisey," he whispered, "do you know what Jesus said to Peter and Andrew?"

I was surprised. Daddy knew the Bible, but we had never spent a lot of time sitting around discussing the New Testament.

"Why, yes," I said slowly. Daddy loved fishing, so maybe it made sense that he'd be thinking about the disciples who were fishermen. "I remember. Jesus told Peter and Andrew to follow Him, and that He would make them fishers of men. And so they left their nets and followed Him."

"That's right," he said, smiling. "Fishers of men."

Those were the last words my father said to me. Hospice nurses say that dying people often speak in metaphors to signal to the living that they're about to pass on, and I realized from my dad's words that death wasn't threatening to him. A lifelong fisherman, he was simply preparing for his journey across the last great river, smiling at Jesus and thinking about fishing for men. It was a great comfort to me.

There was no place for us to sleep in intensive care, so later that night we prepared to go home for a few hours. I went to my childhood home with my mother and fell into bed. At 1 AM the phone rang. "Your father isn't responding," the nurse told me. "I think you'd better come to the hospital."

I helped my mother get ready, and we drove quickly through Newnan's dark streets. My sister met us at the hospital. We sat with Daddy, holding his hands, rubbing his head, letting him know that we were there with him, even though he could not respond.

The attending nurse encouraged us to tell Daddy whatever we needed to say to him, for it would be our last chance. I was so thankful that God had chosen to answer my frequent prayer that Daddy would not die alone. As sad as it was to realize that this was the end, I was also grateful that God was choosing to take him before he became bedridden. I pulled a chair as close as I could to his bedside so that I could hold his warm hand. I knew it would soon be cold.

After about four hours his respiration changed. I knew it was time to tell my mother the truth that I had kept from her for the last few hours. I bent down beside her chair and tried to comfort and prepare her for what was coming, just as she had so often done for me.

"Mama," I said, "the nurse says that Daddy is not going to wake up. His breathing will get more and more shallow, and then his heart will stop. It won't be long now."

My heart broke as I heard my mother pleading with the nurse. "Are you sure?" she kept asking. "Are you sure he's not going to come out of this? Isn't there anything else you can do?"

As Jane and I sat holding our daddy's hands, our mother bent over him, speaking tenderly into his ear and smoothing his hair. I heard her say all the things to him that I had so longed to hear my parents tell each other back when I was a child.

"I have loved you all my life," my silver-haired mother told Daddy, her tears falling on his wrinkled cheek. "You have been a good daddy to your children. You have been such a good husband. I love you."

Then, as dawn broke and a new day began, my father slipped away. I imagined him talking with Peter and Andrew firsthand, swapping fishing stories.

An ending . . . and a new beginning.

A Love That Lasted

Almost seventy years earlier, when my father was twenty-three and my mother was sixteen, they had met at a gas station, introduced by mutual friends. My dad was interested enough to ask my mother if he could see her again.

"I'll be singing at church tonight," my mother said. "If you want to see me again, come there!"

He showed up at church for the service that evening, and my mother's sweet soprano captured his heart. They married, and many years later, when I was a tiny girl, I remember my mother singing solos at church. Forty-something years after that, right before my father's death, my friend Ame was digging through the church archives and found old tape recordings of my mother's melodies. So at Daddy's funeral service, we played my mother singing, from back in 1965, "When God Is Near" and "When Jesus Comes."

As I sat in the church service and listened to my mother's young voice singing those old hymns, it felt like I was outside time for a moment. The music reminded me of when I was five years old and my daddy was invincible, the tireless worker who overcame all kinds of tough obstacles to provide for his family.

I was older now, a mother myself. My mother was now a widow, and my daddy lay still in a casket. It was so strange.

As the service closed, we all listened to another special recording. Alan had known that he wouldn't be able to sing at the funeral without breaking down, and so he'd gone into the studio the day after my father's death and recorded a song with only his longtime producer, Keith Stegall, accompanying him on piano.

"Through death into life everlasting/ He passed, and we follow Him there," Alan sang. "Turn your eyes upon Jesus, look full on His wonderful face . . ."

The Place That Shaped Me

The long, black limousine drove us to my parents' house from the county cemetery where we buried my daddy, near the stone that marks my brother Ron's grave. As we passed through the streets of Newnan, I thought back on the memories of my hometown.

There was the Dairy Queen where Alan and I had met . . . the high school where I had cheered . . . the church where we were married. Here were our parents' homes, where we'd eaten countless Sunday dinners and celebrated birthdays, births, and weddings. The familiar places in this little town were as much a part of me as my accent, my opinions, and my tastes. Here is where I had started to become *me*. As Alan's old song once put it, "where I come from" is the place that had shaped me for as long as I had known. These were my roots.

But as I reflected on my origins in those sweet-sad days after my father's death, I knew that I had deeper roots as well. I remembered Mama Jack, my daddy's mother. My grandfather died when my father was young, but Mama Jack lived past her hundredth birthday. When I was little, she was a short, plump woman with bright blue eyes and long, silver hair that she wore twisted into a bun. She had a well-worn black leather Bible, and even in her nineties, she read through it again and again, without the need for glasses.

"You have been my refuge," the thin, wrinkled page read in my grandmother's book of Psalms. "You have given me the heritage of those who fear your name."[1] I could see that some of the blessings I was receiving, even in the aftermath of my father's death, were because of my grandmother's faith. What she had prayed for her descendents was creating a legacy of faith that would be passed to the next generations. I thought about Mama Jack's sweet, devout spirit . . . and I purposed to spend more time sinking my roots down into the Bible that she had so treasured.

Her prayers had shaped me. I had a legacy of faith as sweet as the old hymns that we sang at family reunions, as dear as my mother's sweet soprano, caught in time, soaring over my father's funeral. It was stronger than the

> I HAD A LEGACY OF FAITH AS SWEET AS THE OLD HYMNS THAT WE SANG AT FAMILY REUNIONS, AS DEAR AS MY MOTHER'S SWEET SOPRANO, CAUGHT IN TIME, SOARING OVER MY FATHER'S FUNERAL.

forces that had shaken me over the years, and it was a heritage I could pass on to my children.

"Your statutes are my heritage forever; they are the joy of my heart," says Psalm 119:111. Before I really got into Bible study, I would have found a statement like that as dry as dust. But over recent years I had turned from regarding the Bible as a boring history book, and started seeing it as an intimate love letter from God to me. The more I got into it, the more it got into me. I found that it was active and alive. It pierced me with its truths, and it had the power to actually change my life.

To change the metaphor, the more I studied God's Word, the more I found hidden treasures that had been there all along, but I hadn't had the eyes to see them before.

Sometimes friends will say, "Well, that's great for you, Denise, but I just don't have any desire at all to study the Bible."

I understand that . . . but what I've found is that when I ask Him, God gives me the feelings I can't drum up on my own. When I just don't want to read God's Word, I pray for Him to give me that craving. I pray that He'll make me want to seek Him, because when we seek God, we can be sure of finding Him.

"You will seek me and find me when you seek me with all your heart," Jeremiah 29:13 says. "I will be found by you" (v. 14). Even after times in my life when I had given my attention to other things, like fame, money, and looking good in other people's eyes, God's promise for me came true. He said, "But if from there you seek the Lord your God, you will find him if you look for him with all your heart and with all your soul."[2] Jesus put it even plainer in the Sermon on the Mount: "Ask and it will be given to you; seek and you will find; knock and the door will be opened to you."[3]

God is not some remote, unknowable force. He can be found, known, and enjoyed. He offers the unique, fulfilling relationship that we all long for, down deep.

I've found that the more I dig into the Bible as His love letter to me, the more I develop a passion for it, and for Him. When my heart is cold and unwilling, I ask Him to change it, and incredibly, He does. As my days unfold, I make sure to schedule uninterrupted time to read God's Word and pray. It's a discipline to do so . . . but when I do it, it fulfills my deepest desires.

Connecting with God

Years ago, if I had a free hour in the afternoon, I would have read a magazine or played tennis or perhaps eaten cheesecake and then gotten on the treadmill. Now, though I still love tennis, reading, and cheesecake (not necessarily in that order), I'm drawn like a magnet to spend even more time with God. When I'm in the car, taking the girls to school or to a basketball or volleyball game, I listen to Christian music . . . though, of course, I also have to get in my time on the country music stations!

Often when I'm in the car, I pray out loud, hoping that anyone who sees my lips moving will just assume I'm talking on a cell phone. One day I felt an odd urgency to pray specifically for a woman named Valerie. Her husband, Scott, the relative of a close friend, had been having some health challenges. It was strange, though, because I felt the urge to pray for Valerie rather than for Scott. Later I found out that at the exact time I was driving along, praying for Valerie, Scott was having a seizure . . . and Valerie was uncharacteristically calm and able to deal with all his needs without panicking.

Throughout the day, in whatever moments I have, I "turn my eyes" onto Jesus by reading the Bible, listening to sermons or uplifting music on CDs, and connecting with friends who share the same passion. The more I focus on Jesus, the more I can fill up with His love and pass that love on to others . . . my family, friends in need, whomever.

That's how it was with my grandmother's love for God's Word. When I was younger I respected her faith, but I didn't really understand it. Now I feel like I've gotten a taste of the great secret she knew, and it makes me hungry for more.

Bible reading and prayer are the ways to really connect with Jesus and develop strong faith. It's not *our* strength, really; it's grafting into *His* strength, like branches of a tree drawing life from the vitality of the trunk and the roots.

This kind of relationship with Jesus isn't dull duty. It's a fun, unpredictable adventure. It's also a paradox: when we're rooted in God, we really begin to go places, places we couldn't have imagined otherwise!

I thought of this when Alan's seventy-six-year-old mother— and her desire for Alan to return to his roots—inadvertently became the incentive for his next platinum album.

Chapter 23

PRECIOUS MEMORIES

⌒◯◯◡

Those who honor Me, I will honor.

from 1 Samuel 2:30

Honor your father and your mother.

Exodus 20:12a

For years Alan's mother had been asking him to record a Gospel album. She brought no pressure or guilt, of course, just the kind of nice, regular reminders by which mothers let their wishes be known.

"I just hope that before I die, you'll make a Gospel CD," Mama Ruth would sigh to her only son. "I know so many people who would just love to hear you sing the great old hymns!"

Alan laughed and teased her and promised he'd do it later. "Don't you worry," he said, stalling. "I'll get around to it someday."

But then Alan saw his mother leave my father's funeral service, with tears streaming down her face after she heard his recording of "Turn Your Eyes upon Jesus." He felt a new urgency to make his mama's Gospel album.

The Family Album

Alan found an old Baptist hymnbook, and we sat down on the hearth by a crackling fire. I got excited as he and I sat and sang the choruses I had loved as a child. I made a short list of thirty of my favorites that I wanted him to do. He politely told me to forget it. "There's no way I'm singin' thirty songs," he said. "People will fall asleep."

In the end he chose fifteen classic songs, which he recorded with wonderful but minimal accompaniment, and with no fancy arrangements, in Keith Stegall's studio. He wanted the old hymns to sound how he remembered them from church in his childhood.

In some ways it was a homespun family project. He asked the girls and me to sing "'Tis So Sweet to Trust in Jesus," and Alan did the album's artwork and photography himself. He found an old, white chapel that looked just like his mother's country church from her childhood, and also shot photographs of our big old family Bible. After he printed the photos, he found that a cross made of light beams was illuminated on the Bible's dark cover.

The CD was finished just before Christmas, and Alan's mother came to join us for the holidays. "Mother," Alan said to her early on Christmas morning, before anyone else was down-stairs, "I want to give you your present now, so you have time to enjoy it."

Mama Ruth sat at our breakfast counter, and Alan turned on the CD. Tears rolled down her cheeks as she heard his voice sounding so much like it had when he sang at church when he was young. She couldn't help but reflect on everything he'd been through. She wept as she thought of the long journey he had made to get to this place of *wanting* to sing those hymns for her, and being able to do so with real conviction in his heart.

My mother was also with us for the holiday. It was her first Christmas without my dad. As she opened my present to her—a quilt made out of scraps of my daddy's old shirts—Alan's CD happened to be playing "When We All Get to Heaven." I smiled as I watched my mother put the soft fabric up to her face, tears in her eyes, and breathe in the faint scent of my father as the music played:

> When we all get to heaven,
> What a day of rejoicing that will be!
> When we all see Jesus,
> We'll sing and shout the victory!

An Unexpected Hit

We made additional copies of Alan's Gospel CD and gave them to extended family and friends. Then, to our surprise, the record label executives decided that our little family CD needed to be released commercially. It was an odd decision. The album wasn't slick or professional. The label wasn't planning to promote it. And they knew that the country radio stations wouldn't play it. In other words, releasing it made no commercial sense. But they did it anyway.

To everyone's surprise, the *Precious Memories* CD shot up the charts and stayed there. Released in February 2006, it spent twelve of its first nineteen weeks at the top of the country, Christian, and Gospel sales charts. It was the first Gospel album ever to debut at #1 on the country music charts. It was #4 on *Billboard's* all-genre 200 sales chart, with *Billboard* calling it "a landmark work" and "a masterpiece." It was one of five nominees for the 2006 "Album of the Year" at the Country Music Awards. It was the top-selling album for 2006 on the Christian music charts. As Reuters news service reported in a year-end story on #1 albums, "Sometimes it's the simplest, purest creative expressions that resonate most powerfully with consumers. The success of Alan Jackson's 'Precious Memories' is a prime example."[1]

After it went platinum, the label had a party, and Alan presented our mothers with generous checks to donate to the charities of their choice. It was fitting that Mother donated hers to the building fund for Unity Baptist Church, the church that I'd grown up in and the sanctuary that my daddy had helped build.

At any rate, no one in the music world could explain just why *Precious Memories* did so well and received so many honors. No one could figure it out at all . . . except maybe Alan's mother. It seems that when God has special plans for something, it will accomplish exactly what He intends—despite the odds against it.

Chapter 24
DRIVE!

⌒∞⌒

Jesus take the wheel
Take it from my hands
Cause I can't do this on my own
I'm letting go
So give me one more chance
To save me from this road I'm on

Brett James, Hillary Lindsey, and
Gordie Sampson, "Jesus Take the Wheel"

I recently read a book in which the author used a metaphor that struck home with me, probably because I live with someone who is crazy about cars. The phases of spiritual growth I've experienced over the last few years are like a journey down the road toward my future.

I'm at the wheel of my imaginary vehicle—let's say it's a white Mustang convertible—and Jesus is in the backseat. This describes the relationship that I had with Him for the first fifteen years of my marriage. Even though in the back of my mind I knew He was there, I didn't think about Him very much, nor did I consider His desires for my life. I was tooling along, listening to the radio, chatting on my cell phone, distracted by many things, hoping I was headed in the right direction. Sometimes I'd feel anxious, like I was driving in a fog and couldn't see what was just ahead of me. Other times I just got lost.

Maybe you've been in this situation. You may have accepted Christ as Savior, but that decision hasn't really affected your day-to-day decisions. Or you may believe that God exists, but He seems irrelevant to your everyday experience.

Who's Driving?

As I became involved in Bible study and started going back to church regularly in the mid-1990s, I began to really want to know the One I'd accepted as my Savior back when I was a child. The more I got into the Scriptures, the more I realized that I truly wanted Him to direct my life. I remembered what the Bible said about His will for me even before I was born.

So I invited Him to move to the front seat of my life's imaginary car. The passenger seat.

I wanted to be closer to Jesus and to hear what He had to say about the direction I was going. I wanted His input, because I really did believe that His directions would be the best route for me.

But at the same time, I wasn't ready for Him to have complete control. I was going along just fine in my supposed fairy-tale life and was afraid that He might want me to head in an entirely different direction—one that might not be exactly what I had envisioned. I didn't want any bumpy or difficult roads. As long as I was in control, I could listen to Christ but still make my own decisions, just in case He asked me to become a missionary to Africa.

We rolled along fine with me in the driver's seat. I was happy to have the renewed relationship with Him. I tuned in to radio stations that He liked. I loved the closeness and warmth I felt when He was with me.

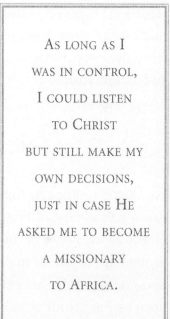

AS LONG AS I WAS IN CONTROL, I COULD LISTEN TO CHRIST BUT STILL MAKE MY OWN DECISIONS, JUST IN CASE HE ASKED ME TO BECOME A MISSIONARY TO AFRICA.

But when Alan left, I couldn't keep the car under control. I had no idea which way to turn. I was totally lost, and I ended up stalled out on the side of the road. Finally I begged Christ to get in the driver's seat, to take complete control. I wanted Him to drive my life, no matter where He'd take me.

In the words of Carrie Underwood's great song, I cried, "Jesus, take the wheel!"

This was scary, but absolutely freeing. I no longer had to figure out where I was going or how I would get there. To continue with the metaphor, Jesus put the top down, and now the wind blows through my hair. Sometimes we stop and pick up people whose spiritual cars have broken down. It's fun. Life has become an open-ended adventure.

I have an idea about where He's taking me on our journey together because I communicate with Him as a friend, but I don't know everything that we'll see or do along the way. He doesn't choose to tell me all the details about where we're headed. But that's fine with me . . . because I trust Him. I know He has great plans for me. I know He has destinations in mind that I never would have been able to find on my own. I've never felt more energized and alive than since I decided to go ahead and let Jesus drive!

Me, Write a Book?

For example, nine years ago the Lord gave me the unlikely desire to write this book. At first, it seemed absurd even to consider it. I had no idea how to begin, no idea how to accomplish it, no idea of the steps to take to make it happen. I'm not a writer, and I'm also just about the last person in the world who would want to open up her life for others to read. I don't like to be exposed.

But God gave me this crazy idea that wouldn't go away. I felt like other people might relate to parts of my story, and that maybe God could use it to draw others to Himself, so they could enjoy His love and freedom too. And eventually, in God's timing, He put together the team to create this book, so I didn't have to go it alone.

Writing a book may not seem like a big deal to someone else. But in this case, and so many others, I'm beginning to learn that with God, nothing is impossible. If I turn everything over to Him, He does for me what I could not do for myself. I'm starting to dream bigger dreams, knowing that I can do everything through Christ who gives me strength.[1]

That doesn't mean I'm suddenly able to leap tall buildings in a single bound. The Bible makes it pretty clear that God gives us the strength to do His will, whatever *He* wants us to do. And while discerning the will of God is a theological topic way beyond the scope of this book, I've found a new connection with His character and His desires for me through spending more deep time in prayer, listening to Him.

Like many Christians, for years I had wanted a more vibrant prayer life. I knew that Bible study and prayer were the keys to real intimacy with Jesus. And though I'd been committed to regular Bible study for several years, my prayer life was sporadic, and often dull or cold.

I know I'm not alone in this. As Philip Yancey writes in *Prayer: Does It Make Any Difference?*, Gallup polls show that nine out of ten Americans pray regularly, and three out of four say that they pray every day. When Yancey interviewed people himself, most said that prayer was very important to them. The rest of the conversation typically went something like this:

"How often do you pray? *Every day.* Approximately how long? *Five minutes—well, maybe seven.* Do you find prayer satisfying? *Not really.* Do you sense the presence of God when you pray? *Occasionally, not often.*"

Yancey says, "Many of those I talked to experience prayer more as a burden than as a pleasure. They regarded it as important, even paramount, and felt guilty about their failure, blaming themselves."[2]

In my own journey with Jesus, a specific set of tools has

revolutionized my prayer life. A friend gave me a book by Becky Tirabassi titled—appropriately—*Let Prayer Change Your Life*. In it Becky describes her own struggles with having a regular and invigorating prayer time, and how God gave her some specific, practical steps that changed it—and her—dramatically. As I engaged in these steps, prayer became an entirely new adventure for me.

I wake up in the mornings with all kinds of wild, random thoughts, but I take comfort that in this I'm like the great writer C. S. Lewis. He said:

> The real problem of the Christian life comes . . . the very moment you wake up each morning. All your wishes and hopes for the day rush at you like wild animals. And the first job each morning consists simply in shoving them all back; in listening to that other voice, taking that other point of view, letting that other, larger, stronger, quieter life coming flowing in.[3]

How Can I Know God?

For me, listening to the larger, stronger voice of God starts with reading His Word. I use a Bible reading program that Becky developed. It has readings listed for each day of the year. These are selections from the Old Testament, New Testament, Psalms, and Proverbs.

After slowly reading the Scriptures, I open my mind and heart to what the Holy Spirit might be saying to me. I listen. I turn it over in my mind, kind of like a cow chewing its cud, though I'm not thrilled about comparing myself to a cow.

Then I get out the prayer journal. It has neat, organized sections in which to jot my prayers.

- In the *praise* section, I often rewrite praises from the Psalms in my own words, to give God the glory that He deserves.

- Next I *admit* my sins to God, jotting down whatever He brings to mind and asking for His forgiveness so my relationship with Him can be current, without any old baggage or garbage between us. Sometimes God brings to mind things for which I need to ask other people to forgive me. For example, the other day in the car, nine-year-old Dani continued to argue with me about something after I had told her to stop. Frustrated, I got very upset with her and reacted with anger. During my prayer time, I realized that I needed to go back and ask her forgiveness for my lack of self-control. So I did!

- In the *request* section, I write down my concerns and requests for myself and others. It has been incredibly rewarding to look back at these journal pages and see all the prayers that God has answered. Some answers have been those I asked for; others have been way outside the box of my own expectations.

- The next section is for *giving thanks* to God. The more I write on these pages, the more comes to mind. Gratitude to God perpetuates more gratitude. It's addictive!

- In the *listening* section, I write whatever I feel the Holy Spirit is saying to me. It might be a certain Scripture that I read that day, or perhaps a new sense of God's guidance in a particular situation. Or something may come to mind that I feel the Lord is leading me to do that day.

• Lastly, I write down anything from the Scripture readings that I want to memorize or apply in a particular way.

My grandmother had her own disciplines for spending time with God in prayer; my daughters may well have different ways that they do it. But for me, this system has been enormously helpful. What is important is not the particular format, but the priority of time reserved for connecting with God. The more we seek Him out, the more we're drawn to be like Him—and the more we're at peace as we see His direction in our lives.

In a world so full of troubles and turns on life's road, prayer really is the believer's key to peace with God. For me, it's the only way I can continue to stay in the passenger seat, where I belong, and make sure that *Jesus* is at the wheel of my life.

Chapter 25

HAPPILY EVER AFTER,
EVEN WHEN WE'RE NOT

In this world you will have trouble.
But take heart! I have overcome the world.

John 16:33b

Two old people without a thing
Children gone but still they sing
Side by side in that front porch swing
Livin' on love
He can't see anymore
And she can barely sweep the floor
Hand in hand they'll walk through that door
Livin' on love

Alan Jackson, "Livin' on Love,"

On a crisp fall evening last year, Alan and I stood at the edge
of the football field at our daughters' high school, feeling like

we were about eighty years old. It was Mattie's homecoming game, and her classmates had elected her as a member of the homecoming court. At her school, these class representatives tend to be not only beautiful young women, but also good students, who show leadership abilities and strong character. We were proud of Mattie for being recognized in this way.

No matter how much we can romanticize relationships, fulfillment, and the future when we're teenagers, real love stories play out much longer, and with a lot more complexity, than a two-and-a-half-minute song on the radio.

At halftime, we climbed down from the stands and stood in front of the chain-link fence adjacent to the field. The band played, and blue and white balloons and banners lined the playing field. The announcer called out the girls' names as they perched on the backs of convertibles proceeding slowly around the field.

"And the sophomore class representative is Miss Mattie Jackson!" he said. Alan and I whooped, clapped, and took several million pictures as Mattie and her escort, Michael, got out of the car and took their places in a semicircle with the rest of the homecoming court.

As I watched Mattie with her long, coral dress and her dark hair gleaming in the lights of the football stadium, I was suddenly struck by a sense of déjà vu, or time travel, or both. I remembered so clearly when I was Mattie's age, standing in the bright lights, my whole life in front of me. Alan had been my escort all those years ago . . . and now here we were, hanging on to the fence in the stadium while our daughter experienced her own high school rite of passage.

I looked up at Alan, and back at Mattie, and thought how very strange life is. No matter how much we romanticize relationships, fulfillment, and the future when we're teenagers, real love stories play out much longer, and with a lot more complexity, than a two-and-a-half-minute song on the radio.

Fairy Tales and Real Life?

In real life the fairy tale is different from the simple version we dream of when we're young. In real life the prince and princess don't just put on the glass slipper, or get rid of the evil step-mother or the villain, and then it's happily ever after. As Alan's very first #1 record put it, "The boy don't always get the girl/here in the real world."

In real life, heroes and heroines go through all kinds of struggles, trouble, and heartaches. If they don't die young, they get wrinkles and lose their hair. They laugh and cry together over decades. They break each other's hearts and help each other heal. Real love matures. It means having to say you're sorry. Real love is deeper, wilder, and stronger than the two-hour romances we see at the movies.

I'm just beginning to learn about that kind of real love. I

haven't figured it all out, and even if I had, I still wouldn't be able to live it, day in and day out. I practice "real love" imperfectly, at best.

But that's where I find real life in my relationship with Jesus so absolutely freeing. I don't have to be perfect. I can't be perfect. But I know that He is with me, forgiving me when I fail and picking me up when I fall. And because of His presence and power with me, I can begin to be the wife, mother, daughter, and friend that I was truly designed to be. When it's all about Him, then our stories not only have an unbelievably happy ultimate ending, but every chapter—happy *or* sad—is somehow sweeter than the one before.

Time for Dessert

I once heard a story about an elderly lady who went to her young pastor to plan her funeral arrangements. I don't know exactly where this took place, but it sounds like the South to me.

The woman listed her choice of hymns, Scripture selections, and exactly what outfit she wanted to wear in her open casket. The pastor, smiling, took careful notes.

"There's one more thing," the lady said.

"What is it, Mrs. Jones?" the pastor asked. "I'll do whatever I can to honor your wishes."

"I want you to make sure that the funeral home takes care of one final arrangement," she said, tapping her cane on the floor for emphasis. "I want them to put me in my casket with a silver fork in my hand."

"A fork?" the pastor repeated.

"Yes," she said. "A sterling silver dessert fork. And when everyone comes and looks in the casket to pay their respects, and they say, 'Why in the world does she have a dessert fork in her hand?' I want you to tell them the reason why."

"And what might that reason be?" the pastor asked, scratching his head.

The elderly woman smiled. "Son, when I was young, my parents told me to eat up my dinner because the best part of the meal was yet to come. We always looked forward to dessert, knowing it would be sweet.

"So I want you to tell those people that I was buried with a dessert fork in my hand because I knew that after this life comes the sweetest part of all. Tell them I knew that by God's grace, *the best is yet to come!*"

I don't think I want to be buried with a dessert fork in my hand, but I agree with the lady in this story. I've learned that all kinds of troubles will come in this life. Jesus said to expect them. They're not the exception; they're the norm. Today's world simmers with terrors and unrest, and our personal lives can churn with hard times too.

But I'm learning that I don't have to be afraid or anxious when the crises come. God is with me. He will give me whatever I need to get through life's challenges. He can do miracles in me, right in the midst of troubled times.

And, whatever happens, *He* is writing our life story. If we yield to His control, we can have peace as our story unfolds. We can have confidence and a sweet sense of anticipation that all *will* be well in the end, when we're enjoying His pleasures forever. The Bible promises, "No eye has seen, no ear has heard, no mind has conceived what God has prepared for those who love him."[1]

To be sure, the very best is yet to come!

Reflection

❦

I don't know where you are on your journey of faith. Maybe you're at the steering wheel of your life's car. Maybe Jesus is in the backseat, or the passenger seat, and you're realizing that you need to ask Him to take the wheel. Or maybe Jesus isn't even in your car, but He's by the side of the road, calling out to you that there is danger ahead.

If you've never really had a relationship with God, and are interested, here are a few things to think about.

First, it's God who stirs our hearts to seek Him. If you find yourself wanting to know God, then the Holy Spirit is moving in your life, like a gentle wind, refreshing you and drawing you to Christ.

The wind blows wherever it pleases.
You hear its sound, but you cannot tell where it comes from or where it is going.

So it is with everyone born of the Spirit.
(John 3:8)

Second, there's some bad news. The bad news is that human beings are sinful. The Bible says that *all* of us have sinned, violating God's absolute standards of pure perfection. Even the very best of us is spiritually contaminated . . . and so we can't connect with an utterly clean, holy God. Not only that, sin's fair consequence is death: spiritual death and separation from God.

All have sinned and fall short of the glory of God.
(Romans 3:23)

For the wages of sin is death,
but the gift of God is eternal life in Christ Jesus our Lord.
(Romans 6:23)

Third, there's some good news. God chose to rescue us from our natural fate. He loves us and made a way for us to connect with Him. That way is His Son, Jesus Christ. The Bible says that God loved the world so much that He sent Jesus to take the punishment of *our* wrongdoing—so that we could be freed from the sentence of spiritual death.

God demonstrates his own love for us in this:
While we were still sinners, Christ died for us.
(Romans 5:8)

God so loved the world that he gave his one and only Son,

that whoever believes in him shall not perish but have
eternal life.
(John 3:16)

Jesus answered, "I am the way and the truth and the life.
No one comes to the Father, except through Me."
(John 14:6)

Fourth, what can we do? We can receive Christ. "Receiving
Christ" begins with admitting that you are a sinner, and asking
Him to forgive you. Whether you and I appear to have led pretty
good lives, or others see us as vile and filthy through and
through, it really doesn't matter, in terms of our "worthiness."
All of us on the planet are unworthy of God's love and His gift
of eternal life.

But He gives that gift of eternal life freely! All we need to do
is accept it by agreeing with Him about the state of things, believing that Jesus paid the fair penalty for our sins when He died on
the cross, and that He beat death and rose from the dead.

Based on everything we know of God, whether it's a lot or
a little, and everything we know about ourselves, whether it's a
lot or a little, we open our hearts, humbly giving control of our
lives over to Him.

If we claim to be without sin, we deceive ourselves and
the truth is not in us.

If we confess our sins, he is faithful and just and will forgive us our sins and purify us from all unrighteousness.
(1 John 1:8–9)

To all who received him, to those who believed in his name, he gave the right to become children of God. (John 1:12)

Fifth, this is an act of faith. There may well be no drama, bells, whistles, or signs in the sky. You may or may not *feel* any different. But this is about believing that God will do what He says. It's about trusting in Someone we cannot see.

Now faith is being sure of what we hope for and certain of what we do not see. (Hebrews 11:1)

By grace you have been saved, through faith—and this not from yourselves, it is the gift of God—not by works, so that no one can boast. (Ephesians 2:8–9)

This righteousness from God comes through faith in Jesus Christ to all who believe. (Romans 3:22)

If you confess with your mouth, "Jesus is Lord," and believe in your heart that God raised him from the dead, you will be saved. (Romans 10:9)

Sixth, if you've prayed and opened your life to Christ, make sure to tell someone! Read the Gospel of Mark or John in the Bible, and connect with a local church, where the Bible is taught and the people love God, so you can grow and be supported in your new faith.

Resources

ere's a list of some of the resources that have been a great help to me in my spiritual journey. There are many more that I haven't listed, but I hope these few might be useful for you.

- The Bible! This is a nonnegotiable, of course. If you don't have a modern translation, get one! I've enjoyed using the New International Version and the New Living Translation.

- Dan Allender, *To Be Told: Know Your Story, Shape Your Future* (Colorado Springs: WaterBrook, 2005).

- Bible Study Fellowship, bsfinternational.org.

- Henry T. Blackaby and Claude V. King, *Experiencing God: How to Live the Full Adventure of Knowing and Doing the Will of God* (Nashville: Broadman & Holman, 1998).

- Community Bible Study, communitybiblestudy.org.

RESOURCES

- C. S. Lewis, *Mere Christianity* (New York: Macmillan, 1943).

- Max Lucado, *A Love Worth Giving* (Nashville: W Publishing, 2006) and *It's Not About Me* (Nashville: Integrity, 2004).

- Beth Moore, Living Proof Ministries, lproof.org.

- Stormie Omartian, *The Power of a Praying Wife* (Eugene, OR.: Harvest House, 1997) and *The Power of a Praying Parent* (Eugene, OR.: Harvest House, 1995).

- Lewis Smedes, *The Art of Forgiving* (New York: Random House, 1996) and *Shame and Grace: Healing the Shame We Don't Deserve* (San Francisco: HarperSanFrancisco, 1994).

- Becky Tirabassi, *My Partner Prayer Notebook, The Change Your Life Daily Bible, Let Prayer Change Your Life, Sacred Obsession.* www.beckytirabassi.com.

- A. W. Tozer, *The Pursuit of God* and *The Knowledge of the Holy* (multiple editions of both available).

- Ellen Vaughn, *Radical Gratitude: Discovering Joy Through Everyday Thankfulness* (Grand Rapids: Zondervan, 2005) and *Time Peace: Living Here and Now with a Timeless God* (Grand Rapids: Zondervan, 2007).

- Philip Yancey, *Prayer: Does It Make Any Difference?* (Grand Rapids: Zondervan, 2006).

About the Authors

A former flight attendant and elementary school teacher, **Denise Jackson** currently delights in devoting most of her time to her husband, country music superstar, Alan Jackson, and their three daughters, ages seventeen, fourteen, and ten. In addition to spending time with her family, Denise enjoys playing tennis and is an avid student of the Bible.

Ellen Vaughn is an award-winning author and speaker. Her works of fiction include *The Strand* and *Gideon's Torch*, which she coauthored with Chuck Colson. She collaborated with Colson on eight other nonfiction books. Vaughn's recent solo works include *Radical Gratitude* and *Time Peace*. Former vice president of executive communications for Prison Fellowship, Vaughn speaks frequently at Christian conferences and has been featured at writers' seminars in the U.S. and Canada. She and her husband, Lee, live in Virginia with daughter Emily, fifteen, twins Haley and Walker, twelve, and an enormous dog named after C. S. Lewis.

Notes

Chapter 14
Letting Go
1. Matt. 13:31–32
2. Mark 9:17–24

Chapter 15
Praying New Prayers
1. Max Lucado, *A Love Worth Giving* (Nashville: W Publishing Group, 2002).

Chapter 17
Coming Home
1. See Stormie Omartian, *The Power of a Praying Wife* (Eugene, Oreg.: Harvest House, 1997).

2. Here are some of the biblical sources for those "downloads":

- "I have loved you with an everlasting love; I have drawn you with loving-kindness. I will build you up again" (Jer. 31:3–4a).

- "'For I know the plans I have for you,' declares the LORD, 'plans to prosper you and not to harm you, plans to give you hope and a future. Then you will call upon me and come and pray to me, and I will listen to you. You will seek me and find me when you seek me with all your heart. I will be found by you,' declares the

LORD, 'and will bring you back from captivity'" (Jer. 29:11–14a).

- "See, I am doing a new thing! Now it springs up; do you not perceive it? I am making a way in the desert and streams in the wasteland" (Isa. 43:19).

- "'My grace is sufficient for you, for my power is made perfect in weakness.' Therefore I will boast all the more gladly about my weaknesses, so that Christ's power may rest on me. That is why, for Christ's sake, I delight in weaknesses, in insults, in hardships, in persecutions, in difficulties. For when I am weak, then I am strong" (2 Cor. 12:9–10).

- "Then Jesus came to them and said, 'All authority in heaven and on earth has been given to me. Therefore go and make disciples of all nations, baptizing them in the name of the Father and of the Son and of the Holy Spirit, and teaching them to obey everything I have commanded you. And surely I am with you always, to the very end of the age'" (Matt. 28:18–20).

Chapter 18
A Hard Road
1. Phil. 4:6–7.
2. Luke 7:37.
3. Luke 7:47.
4. "For as high as the heavens are above the earth, so great is

his love for those who fear him; as far as the east is from the west, so far has he removed our transgressions from us" (Ps. 103:11–12).

5. For the Christian, forgiving another human being has to be considered in light of God's forgiveness of *us*. We learn how to forgive by imitating what God has done in our own lives. I don't think I would have been able to let go of hurt and rage if I hadn't felt such an overwhelming sense of God's pardon of my sins, over and over again. "God is the original, master forgiver," theologian Lewis Smedes wrote. "Each time we grope our reluctant way through the minor miracle of forgiving, we are imitating his style. I am not at all sure that any of us would have had imagination enough to see the possibilities in this way to heal the wrongs of this life had he not done it first." Lewis B. Smedes, *The Art of Forgiving: When You Need to Forgive and Don't Know How* (New York: Random House, 1996).

6. 1 John 1:8–10.

Chapter 19
Making New Vows

1. Jer. 29:10b–12 NLT.

2. "That's the Way," words and music by Pat Terry, copyright 1974, Word Music.

3. Martha Beck, "Shame! Embarrassment! Humiliation!" *O* magazine, May 2004.

4. Ibid.

5. Heb. 12:2, italics added

Chapter 21
What Really Matters

1. Alanna Nash, "Alan Jackson," *USA Weekend*, November 3, 2002.

2. Ibid.

3. See Dan Allender, *To Be Told* (Colorado Springs: Waterbrook, 2005), particularly chapter 3, "What Makes a Good Story?—A Better Way to Read Your Tragedies."

4. Ibid

Chapter 22
Roots
1. Ps. 61:3a, 5b.

2. Deut. 4:29.

3. Mat. 7:7.

Chapter 23
Precious Memories
1. Reuters, "Alan Jackson a Christian Crossover Star," 25 December 2006.

Chapter 24
Drive!
1. Phil. 4:13.

2. Philip Yancey, *Prayer: Does It Make Any Difference?* (Grand Rapids: Zondervan, 2006), 14.

3. C. S. Lewis, *Mere Christianity* (New York: Macmillan, 1979), 168–69.

Chapter 25
Happily Ever After, Even When We're Not
1. 1 Cor. 2:9.

SPECIAL EDITION CD
INCLUDED IN THIS BOOK
By ALAN JACKSON
IT'S ALL ABOUT HIM and **THAT'S THE WAY**
Produced by Keith Stegall
Recorded and Mixed by Gary Paczosa
Assisted by Brandon Bell, Greg Lawrence &
    Steve Crowder
Additional Engineering by Matt Rovey
Recorded at Emerald Studios, Minutia and Ocean
Way Studios, Nashville, TN
Mastered by Hank Williams at MasterMix,
    Nashville, TN
Production Coordinator: Jason Campbell
Eddie Bayers – Drums
Brent Mason – Electric Guitar
Glenn Worf – Bass
Bruce Watkins – Acoustic Guitar
Paul Franklin – Steel Guitar
Stuart Duncan – Fiddle
Gary Prim – Piano & Keyboards
John Wesley Ryles – Background Vocals
Lisa Cochran – Background Vocals
On "It's All About Him"
Brass and Choir arranged by Kristin Wilkinson and
Larry Paxton.
Copyist: Stephen Lamb
Percussion: Sam Bacco
Uileann Pipes, Harmonium & Penny Whistle: John
Mock
Trombone/Euphonium: Barry Green
Trombone/Bass Trombone: Prentiss Hobbs
French Horn: Beth Beeson, Erin Houser & Radu
Rusu
Trumpet: Steve Patrick & Jim Williamson
Tuba: Joe Murphy
Choir: Jon Mark Ivey, Terry White, Kirk Kirkland,
Duane Hamilton, Travis Cottrell, Stephanie Hall,
Shelley Jennings, Missy Hale, Nirva Ready, Lisa
Bevill, Vicki Hampton, Melodie CrittendenForward
I'D LOVE YOU ALL OVER AGAIN
By ALAN JACKSON
© 1990 (Renewed) WB MUSIC CORP.
All Rights Reserved Used by Permission of
    ALFRED PUBLISHING CO., INC.

Chapter 1 & 25 (inside)
LIVIN' ON LOVE
Words and Music by ALAN JACKSON
© 1995 WB MUSIC CORP.

All rights Reserved Used by Permission of
    ALFRED PUBLISHING CO., INC.

Chapter 2
LITTLE BITTY
Words and Music by TOM T. HALL
©1996 SONY/ATV SONGS LLC. All rights adminis-
tered by SONY/ATV MUSIC PUBLISHING,
    8 Music Square West, Nashville, TN 37203.
All rights reserved Used by permission

Chapter 3
WHERE I COME FROM
Words and Music by ALAN JACKSON
© 2000 WB MUSIC CORP. and YEE HAW MUSIC
All Right Administered by WB MUSIC CORP
All rights Reserved Used by Permission of
    ALFRED PUBLISHING CO., INC.

Chapter 4
RAINY DAY IN JUNE
Words and Music by ALAN JACKSON
© 2004 EMI APRIL MUSIC INC. and
    TRI-ANGELS MUSIC
All Rights Controlled and Administered by
    EMI APRIL MUSIC INC.
All Rights Reserved
International Copyright Secured
Used by Permission

Chapter 5, 9, 18 & Forward
REMEMBER WHEN
Words and Music by ALAN JACKSON
© 2003 EMI APRIL MUSIC INC. and
    TRI-ANGELS MUSIC
All Rights Controlled and Administered by
    EMI APRIL MUSIC INC.
All Rights Reserved
International Copyright Secured
Used by Permission
Chapter 5 (inside) & 19 (inside)
THAT'S THE WAY
Words and Music by PAT TERRY
© 1976 WORD MUSIC, LLC
All Right Reserved
Used by Permission

Chapter 6
FIRST LOVE
Words and Music by ALAN JACKSON

© 2002 EMI APRIL MUSIC INC. and
TRI-ANGELS MUSIC
All Rights Controlled and Administered by
EMI APRIL MUSIC INC.
All Rights Reserved
International Copyright Secured
Used by Permission

Chapter 7
TO DO WHAT I DO
Words and Music by TIM JOHNSON
© 2004 WARNER-TAMERLANE PUBLISHING
CORP., MARATHON KEY II MUSIC and
TIM JOHNSON PUBLISHING
All Rights on Behalf of itself and MARATHON KEY
II MUSIC Administered by
WARNER-TAMERLANE PUBLISHING CORP.
All rights Reserved
Used by Permission

Chapter 8
THE WAY I AM
Words and Music by SONNY THROCKMORTON
© 1979 SONY/ATV TUNES LLC. All rights
administered by SONY/ATV MUSIC
PUBLISHING, 8 Music Square West,
Nashville, TN 37203.
All rights reserved
Used by permission

Chapter 8 (inside)
HERE IN THE REAL WORLD
Words and Music by ALAN JACKSON and
MARK IRWIN
© 1990 WB MUSIC CORP. and
TEN TEN TUNES (ASCAP)
All rights Reserved
Used by Permission

Chapter 10
LIFE OR LOVE
Words and Music by HARLEY ALLEN and
GARY COTTON
© 2002 COBURN MUSIC, INC. (BMI) and © 2000
EMI BLACKWOOD MUSIC, INC., and
SOUND ISLAND PUBLISHING (ASCAP)
All Rights on Behalf of SOUND ISLAND
PUBLISHING
(ASCAP) Administered by COPYRIGHT
SOLUTIONS, PO Box 3390 Brentwood, TN

37204.
All Right Reserved
International Copyright Secured
Used by Permission

Chapter 10 (inside) & 14
TURN YOUR EYES UPON JESUS
Words and Music by HELEN H. LEMMEL
©1922 PUBLIC DOMAIN

Chapter 11
TALL, TALL TREES
Words and Music by GEORGE JONES and
ROGER MILLER
© 1957 by STARRITE PUBLISHING COMPANY
Copyright Renewed and Assigned to FORT KNOX
MUSIC INC. and TRIO MUSIC COMPANY, INC.
All Rights Reserved
International Copyright Secured
Used by Permission

Chapter 12
BLUEBIRD
Words and Music by LEON RUSSELL
© 1975 IRVING MUSIC, INC.
Copyright Renewed
All Rights Reserved
Used by Permission

Chapter 13
A LITTLE BLUER THAN THAT
Words and Music by MARK IRWIN and
IRENE REBECCA KELLEY
(c) 2001 EMI APRIL MUSIC INC. and
IRENE KELLEY MUSIC
All Rights Controlled and Administered by
EMI APRIL MUSIC INC.
All Rights Reserved
International Copyright Secured
Used by Permission

Chapter 16
LEANING ON THE EVERLASTING ARMS
Words by ELISHA A. HOFFMAN
Music by ANTHONY J. SHOWALTER
©1887 PUBLIC DOMAIN

Chapter 17 (inside)
GONE CRAZY
Words and Music by ALAN JACKSON
© 1998 WB MUSIC CORP. and YEE HAW MUSIC

All Rights on Behalf of YEE HAW MUSIC
Administered by WB MUSIC CORP.
All rights Reserved
Used by Permission of ALFRED PUBLISHING CO.,
    INC.

Chapter 17 & 18
SOFTLY AND TENDERLY
Words and Music by WILL L. THOMPSON
© 1880 PUBLIC DOMAIN

Chapter 20
WORK IN PROGRESS
Words and Music by ALAN JACKSON
© 2002 EMI APRIL MUSIC INC. and
    TRI-ANGELS MUSIC
All Rights Controlled and Administered by
    EMI APRIL MUSIC INC.
All Rights Reserved
International Copyright Secured
Used by Permission

Chapter 21
WHERE WERE YOU
(WHEN THE WORLD STOPPED TURNING)
Words and Music by ALAN JACKSON
© 2001 EMI APRIL MUSIC INC. and
    TRI-ANGELS MUSIC
All Rights Controlled and Administered by
    EMI APRIL MUSIC INC.
All Rights Reserved
International Copyright Secured
Used by Permission

Chapter 21 (inside)
LET IT BE CHRISTMAS
Words and Music by ALAN JACKSON
(c) 2002 EMI APRIL MUSIC INC. and
    TRI-ANGELS MUSIC
All Rights Controlled and Administered by
    EMI APRIL MUSIC INC.
All Rights Reserved
International Copyright Secured
Used by Permission

Chapter 23
JESUS TAKE THE WHEEL
Words and Music by BRETT JAMES,
    GORDIE SAMPSON and HILLARY LINDSEY
© 2005 SONY/ATV TUNES LLC, DIMENSIONAL
    MUSIC OF 1091, STAGE THREE SONGS,
    CORNMAN MUSIC, MUSIC OF WINDSWEPT,
    1609 SONGS, NO SUCH MUSIC, PASSING
    STRANGER MUSIC and RAYLENE MUSIC.
All Rights on behalf of SONY/ATV TUNES LLC
Administered by SONY/ATV MUSIC PUBLISHING,
    8 Music Square West, Nashville, TN 37203
All Rights on behalf of DIMENSTIONAL MUSIC
    OF 1091 Administered by CHERRY LANE
MUSIC PUBLISHING COMPANY, INC.
All Rights on behalf of CORNMAN MUSIC
Administered by STAGE THREE SONGS
All Rights on behalf of 1609 SONGS,
    NO SUCH MUSIC and PASSING STANGER
MUSIC Administered by MUSIC OF WINDSWEPT
All Rights on behalf of RAYLENE MUSIC
    Administered by BPJ ADMINISTRATION,
    P.O. Box 218061, Nashville, TN 37221-8061
All Rights on behalf of STAGE THREE SONGS
    Administered by STAGE THREE MUSIC (US), Inc.
All Rights Reserved
International Copyright Secured
Used by Permission

Chapter 23 (Inside)
WHEN WE ALL GET TO HEAVEN
Words by ELIZA E. HEWITT and Music by
    EMILY D. WILSON
©1898 PUBLIC DOMAIN